WITH WORKBOOK

English for Today's World

2B

WITH WORKBOOK

TOP NOTCH

English for Today's World

2B

Joan Saslow ■ Allen Ascher

With *Top Notch Pop Songs and Karaoke*
by Rob Morsberger

PEARSON
Longman

Top Notch: English for Today's World   2B with Workbook

Pearson Education, 10 Bank Street, White Plains, NY 10606

Editorial director: Pamela Fishman
Senior development editors: Martin Yu, Trish Lattanzio
Development editor: Geraldine Geniusas
Associate development editors: Siobhan Sullivan, Judy Li
Vice president, director of design and production: Rhea Banker
Director of electronic production: Aliza Greenblatt
Managing editor: Mike Kemper
Production editor: Michael Mone
Art director: Ann France
Senior manufacturing buyer: Dave Dickey
Photo research: Aerin Csigay
Digital layout specialist: Warren Fischbach
Text composition: Kirchoff-Wohlberg, Word & Image Design Studio, Inc.
Text font: Palatino 11/13, Frutiger 10/12
Cover photograph: "From Above," by Rhea Banker. Copyright © 2005 Rhea Banker.

Photo credits: All original photography by David Mager. Page 65 (chocolates) Renee Comet Photography/Stockfood America, (sardines) Maximilian Stock/Stockfood America, (shellfish) Geoffrey Clifford/Woodfin Camp Associates, (tofu) Gary Conner/PhotoEdit, (steak) Renee Comet Photography/Stockfood America, (noodles) Alan Campbell Productions/Stockfood America, (fries) Maximilian Stock/Stockfood America; p. 66 (sushi) Vito Arcomano/eStock Photo, (mango) Dorey Cardinale Photography/Stockfood America, (ice cream) Judd Pilossof/FoodPix, (pasta) Thom DeSanto Photography, Inc./Stockfood America, (asparagus) Andy Ryan Photography/Stockfood America; p. 68 Dave King/Dorling Kindersley; p. 69 Digital Visoin Ltd.; p. 70 (A left) Cathy Melloan/PhotoEdit, (A right) Gary White Photography/Stockfood America, (B left) Jimmy Dorantes/LatinFocus.com, (B right) George D. Lepp/Corbis, (C) Steve Cohen/FoodPix, (D) David Young-Wolff/PhotoEdit, (E) Foodcollection/Stockfood America, (F) Michael Newman/PhotoEdit; p. 71 Stephen Hayward/Dorling Kindersley; p. 73 (background) Tyson Foods, Inc., (US) Spathias & Miller/Stockfood America, (China) John E. Kelly/FoodPix, (Brazil) Michael Newman/PhotoEdit, (Korea) James Baigrie/FoodPix, (Vietnam) Steven Mark Needham/FoodPix, (Venezuela) Renee Comet Photography/Stockfood America, (Mexico) Jimmy Dorantes/LatinFocus.com; p. 75 Bob Elsdale/Getty Images; p. 76 Photolibrary.com; p. 77 (top left to right) Leslye Borden/PhotoEdit, Troy Wayrynen/Columbian/NewSport/Corbis, eStock Photo, Corbis Digital Stock, (middle left to right) Setboun/Corbis, Corbis Digital Stock, Neal & Molly Jansen/SuperStock, Image Source/ImageState; p. 79 Dorling Kindersley; p. 80 David Butlow/Corbis; p. 81 (top) David Muir/Masterfile, (bottom) Getty Images; p. 83 (top) Jerry Tobias/Corbis, (left) Tony Freeman/PhotoEdit, (right) Anthony Redpath/Corbis, (bottom) Ken Weingart/ImageState; p. 86 (top left) Historical Picture Archive/Corbis, (bottom left) O'Keeffe, Georgia (1887-1986). "White Flower on Red Earth, #1". 1943. Oil on canvas, 26" x 30 1/4". Inv.: 46.157. The Newark Museum/Art Resource, NY; p. 88 Francis G. Mayer/Corbis; p. 89 (Accademia) Alinari Archives/Corbis, (David) Copyright © 2001 by Martin Yu, (Palace) Bohemian Nomad Picturemakers/Corbis, (Kuan) Fan Kuan, Chinese. Travelers among Mountains and Streams, c. 1000. Hanging scroll, ink and colors on silk, 81 1/4" L. Collection of the National Palace Museum, Taiwan, Republic of China, (Louvre) Richard List/Corbis, (da Vinci) Gianni Dagli Orti/Corbis; p. 90 (glass) Susan Van Etten/PhotoEdit, (silver) Charles Edensaw (c. 1839-1924). Silver bracelet (eagle design), c. 1890. Coin silver. Native American, Haida. Diam. 2 1/2"; H. 1 3/16". Accession number 91.1.130. Gift of John H. Hauberg. Photograph by Paul Macapia. Seattle Art Museum, (gold) Art Resource, NY, (clay) Stockbyte, (wood) Heini Schneebeli/The Bridgeman Art Library International Ltd., (stone) Corbis, (cloth) Keren Su/Corbis, (chair) Victoria & Albert Museum, London/Art Resource, NY, (figure) The Art Archive/Egyptian Museum Turin/Jacqueline Hyde/Picture Desk, (vase) The Art Archive/Museo Vetriano de Murano/Dagli Orti(A)/Picture Desk, (bowl) Banco Mexicano de Imaagenes/The Bridgeman Art Library International Ltd., (bag) David Young-Wolff/PhotoEdit, (figure) Sakamoto Photo Research Laboratory/Corbis; p. 91 (dolls) Dave G. Houser/Corbis, (vase Korea) Corbis, (gold figure) Mireille Vautier/Woodfin Camp & Associates, (vase France) The Art Archive/Dagli Orti(A)/Picture Desk, (stone figure) Claudia Obrocki/Art Resource, NY, (wood figure) Paul A. Souders/Corbis; p. 92 Photos of Yu Gan, Yu Heng, and Yu Kuai courtesy of Yu Gan; p. 93 Dorling Kindersley; p. 94 (background) Marcel Bekken/Fotopersbureau Noordoost, (portrait) Giraudon/Art Resource, (Arles) Damir Frkovic/Masterfile, (vase) Art Resource, NY; p. 95 (Rodin) Hulton Archive/Getty Images, (Lee) Reuters NewMedia Inc./Corbis, (Versace) Rune Hellestad/Corbis, (brush) Tim Ridley/Dorling Kindersley, (Salgado) Vincenzo Pinto/Corbis, (Cassat) Culver Pictures, Inc., (Gehry) AP Wide World Photos; p. 96 (A) Collier Campbell Lifeworks/Corbis, (B) Archivo Iconografico, S.A./Corbis, (C) Art Resource, NY, (D) Art Resource, (E) The Art Archive/Museo del Oro Bogota/Dagli Orti(A)/Picture Desk, (F) Erich Lessing/Art Resource, NY; p. 97 (background) Chris Orr/Dorling Kindersley, (National) Wolfgang Kaehler/Corbis, (Eyck) Jan van Eyck (c. 1390-1441), The Portrait of Giovanni, Arnolfini and his Wife Giovanna Cenami. The Arnolfini Marriage, 1434 oil on panel. National Gallery, London, UK/Bridgeman Art Library, (Victoria) Sandro Vannini/Corbis, (Luck) Art Resource, NU, (Tate) Paul Solomon/Woodfin Camp & Associates, (British) Macduff everton/Corbis, (Mustard) Roy Lichtenstein, Mustard on White. 1963. Magnacolour on plexiglass. 80 x 94 x 5.1 cm. Lent from a private collection. Tate Gallery, London. (c) Tate Gallery, London/Art Resource, NY. (c) Estate of Roy Lichtenstein, (Discus) Scala/Art Resource, NY; p. 98 (monitor) Burke/ Triolo/Getty Images, (mic) Getty Images, (head) Logitech, Inc., (speakers) Logitech, Inc., (drive) Corbis Digital Stock, (keyboard) Logitech, Inc., (games) Frank LaBua/Pearson Education/PH College, (joy) Logitech, Inc., (soft) Frank LaBua/Pearson Education/PH College; p. 99 Courtesy Epson America, Inc. & Mercier Wimberg Photography; p. 100 Images.com/Corbis; p. 101 Logitech, Inc., p. 103 PalmOne, Inc.; p. 105 Nicholas Eveleigh/SuperStock; p. 110 (middle) Getty Images; p. 111 Richard Cummins/Corbis; p. 113 (wallet) Steve Gorton/Dorling Kindersley, (glove) Clive Streeter/Dorling Kindersley, (jacket) Steve Gorton & Andy Crawford/Dorling Kindersley, (suitcase) Dorling Kindersley, (phone) Dorling Kindersley, (books) Myrleen Ferguson Cate/PhotoEdit; p. 116 (top) Robert Rathe/Mira.com, (middle) Catherine Karnow/Corbis, (bottom) Jeffrey Allan Salter/Corbis; p. 117 Library of Congress; p. 118 (background) Ken Ross/Getty Images; p. W53 Getty Images; p. W66 Index Stock Imagery; p. W68 (1) Heini Schneebeli/The Bridgeman Art Library International Ltd., (2) Stockbyte, (3) Dave G. Houser/Corbis, (4) The Art Archive/Dagli Orti(A)/Picture Desk, (5) The Art Archive/Egyptian Museum Turin/Jacqueline Hyde/Picture Desk, (6) Banco Mexicano de Imaagenes/The Bridgeman Art Library International Ltd., (7) David Young-Wolff/PhotoEdit, (8) Art Resource, NY; p. W70 Bettmann/Corbis; p. W72 (left to right) Heini Schneebeli/The Bridgeman Art Library International Ltd., The Art Archive/Dagli Orti(A)/Picture Desk, Tony Freeman/PhotoEdit, Banco Mexicano de Imaagense/The Bridgeman Art Library International Ltd., Stockbyte, David Young-Wolff/PhotoEdit.

Illustration credits: Steve Attoe, pp. 66, 82, 104, 111, W50, W51, W64, W78, W86, W87 (top), W90; John Ceballos, pp. 85, 109, 121; Mark Collins, p. 87; Leanne Franson, pp. W56, W87 (bottom); Brian Hughes, pp. 62, 71, 118; Stephen Hutchings, p. W57; Suzanne Mogensen, pp. W49, W55; Andy Myer, pp. 64, 106; Dusan Petriçic, pp. 70, 78, 79, 115, W88, W89; Steve Schulman, pp. W68 (bottom), W84; Neil Stewart, pp. 119, W75.

ISBN: 0-13-110492-6 (Student's Book with Workbook and Audio CD)
0-13-223188-3 (Student's Book with Workbook and Take-Home Super CD-ROM)

Printed in the United States of America
15–V051–11

Contents

Scope and Sequence FOR 2A AND 2B

GRAMMAR BOOSTER

UNIT	Vocabulary*	Conversation Strategies	Grammar	
1 **Greetings and Small Talk** *Page 2* *Top Notch* Song: "Greetings and Small Talk"	• Customs around the world • Tourist activities	• Ask <u>What have you been up to?</u> or <u>How have you been?</u> to start a conversation • Add information beyond <u>Yes</u> or <u>No</u> to continue a conversation • Use <u>That's great</u> to shift to a new topic	• The present perfect: <u>yet</u>, <u>already</u>, <u>ever</u>, and <u>before</u> • past participles	• Further explanation of form and usage: the present perfect
2 **Movies and Entertainment** *Page 14* *Top Notch* Song: "Better Late Than Never"	• Explanations for being late • Ways to express likes and dislikes • Movie genres • Adjectives to describe movies	• Use <u>They say</u> to support a suggestion • Use <u>Actually</u> to indicate that what you are about to say may be surprising • Use <u>For real?</u> to convey surprise	• The present perfect: additional uses—<u>for</u> and <u>since</u> • <u>Would rather</u>	• Contrasting the present perfect and the present perfect continuous • Spelling rules for the present participle
3 **Staying at Hotels** *Page 26*	• Telephone messages • Hotel room features • Hotel facilities • Hotel room amenities and services	• Use <u>I'd like to</u> to politely state your purpose on the phone • Use <u>That's right</u> to confirm • Use <u>By the way</u> to introduce a new topic or a question	• The future with <u>will</u> • <u>Had better</u>	• Further explanation of usage: future with <u>will</u> and <u>be going to</u> • Degrees of obligation: <u>have to</u>, <u>must</u>, <u>had better</u>, <u>be supposed to</u>, <u>should</u>, <u>ought to</u>, and <u>could</u>
4 **Cars and Driving** *Page 38* *Top Notch* Song: "Wheels around the World"	• Ways to show concern • Car parts • Types of cars • Bad driving behaviors • Polite address • Phrasal verbs	• Use expressions such as <u>I'm so sorry</u> and <u>How awful</u> to convey concern • Begin a response with <u>Well</u> to introduce an explanation	• The past continuous • Direct object placement with phrasal verbs	• Further explanation of usage: the past continuous • Direct object placement: separable and inseparable phrasal verbs
5 **Personal Care and Appearance** *Page 50*	• Personal care products • Salon services • Ways to schedule and pay for personal care • Ways to improve appearance	• Repeat part of a question before answering to clarify • Use <u>Can I get</u> to make a request more polite	• Count and non-count nouns: indefinite quantities and amounts—<u>some</u>, <u>any</u>, <u>a lot of</u>, <u>many</u>, and <u>much</u> • <u>Someone</u> and <u>anyone</u>	• Review of non-count nouns: containers, quantifiers, and other modifiers • <u>Too many</u>, <u>too much</u>, and <u>enough</u> • Indefinite pronouns: <u>something</u>, <u>anything</u>, and <u>nothing</u>

*In *Top Notch*, the term *vocabulary* refers to individual words, phrases, and expressions.

Speaking	Pronunciation	Listening	Reading	Writing
• Offer to introduce someone • Get reacquainted with someone • Greet a visitor • Talk about tourist activities • Explain local customs • Ask about life experiences	• Negative contractions	• People ask visitors about what they've done Task: identify activities • A game show Task: describe the guests' life experiences • Conversation with a visitor Task: identify tourist sights visited	• Magazine article about gestures around the world • Customs around the world • Experiences survey	• Write about an experience • Create a guide for visitors to your country on how to behave • Introduce yourself
• Apologize for and explain lateness • Offer to pay or return the favor • Compare tastes in movies • Describe movies you've seen lately • Discuss the effects of violence in the media	• Reduction of /h/	• Movie reviews Task: identify genres and recommendations • Two people choose a movie to see Task: write movie descriptions • Conversations about movies Task: use adjectives to describe the movies	• Magazine article about violence in movies • Movie catalog ads • Movie reviews	• Write a movie review page • Express opinions about violence in media
• Leave and take a phone message • Check into and out of a hotel • Discuss hotel room features and facilities • Request housekeeping services • Choose a hotel	• Contractions with will	• Phone calls to a hotel Task: take phone messages • Conversations about hotel reservations Task: write the room features guests want • Requests for hotel room amenities and services Task: identify the services and items requested	• Tourist guide recommending New York hotels • Hotel bill • Hotel preference survey	• Describe the advantages and disadvantages of a hotel • Describe a hotel you've stayed at
• Describe a car accident and damage • Express concern • Ask for service and repairs • Describe car problems • Rent a car • Discuss driving rules	• Stress of particles in phrasal verbs	• People describe car accidents Task: identify car damage • Phone calls to a car rental agency Task: infer if the caller rented the car • Conversations with a car rental agent Task: listen for car types	• Magazine article about driving abroad • Online response to car rental request • International road signs • Driving safety survey	• Compare good and bad drivers
• Shop for personal care products • Ask for something you can't find • Request salon services • Schedule and pay for personal care • Discuss ways people improve their appearance	• Vowel reduction to /ə/	• Radio advertisements Task: identify personal care products • Conversations about salon appointments Task: identify salon services • Customers ask about personal care services Task: listen for the services requested and explain what happened	• Advice column about cosmetic surgery • Personal appearance survey	• Write a letter to a magazine's editor • Describe a personal care product you like

UNIT	Vocabulary	Conversation Strategies	Grammar	
6 **Eating Well** *Page 62*	• Excuses for not eating something • Food passions • Lifestyles and health problems • Describing food	• Use <u>Don't worry about it</u> to decline an apology • Use <u>Well</u> to introduce an opinion that differs from someone else's	• Negative <u>yes</u> / <u>no</u> questions and <u>Why don't</u> …? • <u>Used to</u>	• Further explanation of usage: negative <u>yes</u> / <u>no</u> questions with short answers • Further explanation of usage: <u>Why don't</u> / <u>doesn't</u> …? • Further explanation of form: <u>used to</u>
7 **Psychology and Personality** *Page 74* *Top Notch* Song: "The Colors of Love"	• Describing colors • Adjectives of emotion • Suggestions to cheer someone up • Adjectives to describe personality	• Use <u>You know,</u>... to be less abrupt • Use <u>out of the question</u> to indicate opposition • Use <u>Really?</u> to indicate a difference of opinion • Use <u>Thanks for asking</u> to acknowledge another's concern	• Gerunds and infinitives after certain verbs • Gerunds after prepositions • Expressions with prepositions	• Further explanation of form and usage: gerunds and infinitives • Negative gerunds
8 **Enjoying the Arts** *Page 86* *Top Notch* Song: "To Each His Own"	• Types of art • Common materials • Positive adjectives • Ways to say you don't like something	• Use <u>For one thing</u> to provide one reason among several • Use <u>Excuse me</u> to ask for attention in a store	• The passive voice: statements and questions	• Further explanation of form and usage: the passive voice • The passive voice: intransitive verbs
9 **Living with Computers** *Page 98*	• Computer products and accessories • Computer toolbars and commands • Internet activities	• Use <u>Oh yeah?</u> to show that you are interested • Use <u>Everyone says</u> to solicit an opinion • Use <u>Well</u> to soften a contradictory opinion • Use <u>Why don't you</u> to respectfully offer advice	• Comparisons with <u>as … as</u> • The infinitive of purpose	• Review: comparatives and superlatives • <u>As … as</u> with adverbs • Expressing purpose with <u>in order to</u> and <u>for</u>
10 **Ethics and Values** *Page 110*	• Ways to acknowledge thanks • Ways to express certainty • Moral dilemmas • Personal values	• Use <u>Excuse me</u> to get a stranger's attention • Ask <u>You think so?</u> to probe the wisdom of a course of action	• Possessive pronouns • Factual and unreal conditional sentences	• Further explanation of form and usage: factual and unreal conditional sentences

Speaking	Pronunciation	Listening	Reading	Writing
• Offer dishes and decline food • Talk about foods you love and hate • Discuss lifestyle changes • Describe unique foods	• Used to	• Conversations about food Task: identify excuses for not eating something • Descriptions of food passions Task: determine each person's food passions • Descriptions of unique foods Task: describe food items	• News article about changing lifestyles and obesity • The healthy-eating pyramid • Lifestyle survey	• Write about lifestyle changes • Describe a dish
• State color preferences • Describe your mood and emotions • Cheer someone up • Discuss personatlity types • Discuss the impact of birth order on relationships	• Reduction of to in infinitive phrases	• Conversations about color preferences Task: write color names and adjectives of emotion • An academic lecture Task: infer definitions of personality • Conversations about emotions Task: describe how each speaker feels about certain things	• Magazine article about the impact of birth order on personality • Color survey • Personality survey	• Describe your own personality • Describe the personality of someone you know well
• Recommend a museum • Describe an object • Describe how you decorate your home • Discuss your favorite artists • Express opinions about art	• Emphatic stress	• A biography of Vincent Van Gogh Task: listen for his life events • Conversations about art objects Task: identify the objects discussed	• Magazine article about the role of art in two people's lives • Guide to London museums	• Create a short biography of an artist you like • Describe a piece of art you like
• Discuss buying a computer product • Recommend "a better deal" • Troubleshoot a problem • Describe how you use computers • Discuss the benefits and problems of the Internet	• Stress in as … as phrases	• Conversations about using computers Task: identify computer commands • Descriptions of computer activities Task: listen for things to do on the Internet • Conversations comparing two computer products Task: complete comparative sentences	• Four news articles about serious problems with the Internet • Electronics store website • Consumer information card	• Express your opinion about the social impact of the Internet • Report how you use a computer
• Return lost property • Discuss an ethical choice • Express personal values • Discuss honesty • Warn about consequences	• Assimilation of the sounds /d/ + /y/	• Conversations about personal values Task: identify each person's personal values and infer meaning of key words and phrases	• News article about the Tokyo lost-and-found • Values self-test	• Express opinions about modesty • Write an article about appropriate appearance in your country • Narrate a true story about an ethical choice

Acknowledgments

Top Notch International Advisory Board

The authors gratefully acknowledge the substantive and formative contributions of the members of the International Advisory Board.

CHERYL BELL, Middlesex County College, Middlesex, New Jersey, USA • **ELMA CABAHUG**, City College of San Francisco, San Francisco, California, USA • **JO CARAGATA**, Mukogawa Women's University, Hyogo, Japan • **ANN CARTIER**, Palo Alto Adult School, Palo Alto, California, USA • **TERRENCE FELLNER**, Himeji Dokkyo University, Hyogo, Japan • **JOHN FUJIMORI**, Meiji Gakuin High School, Tokyo, Japan • **ARETA ULHANA GALAT**, Escola Superior de Estudos Empresariais e Informática, Curitiba, Brazil • **DOREEN M. GAYLORD**, Kanazawa Technical College, Ishikawa, Japan • **EMILY GEHRMAN**, Newton International College, Garden Grove, California, USA • **ANN-MARIE HADZIMA**, National Taiwan University, Taipei, Taiwan • **KAREN KYONG-AI PARK**, Seoul National University, Seoul, Korea • **ANA PATRICIA MARTÍNEZ VITE DIP. R.S.A.**, Universidad del Valle de México, Mexico City, Mexico • **MICHELLE ANN MERRITT**, Proulex/ Universidad de Guadalajara, Guadalajara, Mexico • **ADRIANNE P. OCHOA**, Georgia State University, Atlanta, Georgia, USA • **LOUIS PARDILLO**, Korea Herald English Institute, Seoul, Korea • **THELMA PERES**, Casa Thomas Jefferson, Brasilia, Brazil • **DIANNE RUGGIERO**, Broward Community College, Davie, Florida, USA • **KEN SCHMIDT**, Tohoku Fukushi University, Sendai, Japan • **ALISA A. TAKEUCHI**, Garden Grove Adult Education, Garden Grove, California, USA • **JOSEPHINE TAYLOR**, Centro Colombo Americano, Bogotá, Colombia • **PATRICIA VECIÑO**, Instituto Cultural Argentino Norteamericano, Buenos Aires, Argentina • **FRANCES WESTBROOK**, AUA Language Center, Bangkok, Thailand

Reviewers and Piloters

Many thanks also to the reviewers and piloters all over the world who reviewed *Top Notch* in its final form.

G. Julian Abaqueta, Huachiew Chalermprakiet University, Samutprakarn, Thailand • **David Aline**, Kanagawa University, Kanagawa, Japan • **Marcia Alves**, Centro Cultural Brasil Estados Unidos, Franca, Brazil • **Yousef Al-Yacoub**, Qatar Petroleum, Doha, Qatar • **Maristela Barbosa Silveira e Silva**, Instituto Cultural Brasil-Estados Unidos, Manaus, Brazil • **Beth Bartlett**, Centro Colombo Americano, Cali, Colombia • **Carla Battigelli**, University of Zulia, Maracaibo, Venezuela • **Claudia Bautista**, C.B.C., Caracas, Venezuela • **Rob Bell**, Shumei Yachiyo High School, Chiba, Japan • **Dr. Maher Ben Moussa**, Sharjah University, Sharjah, United Arab Emirates • **Elaine Cantor**, Englewood Senior High School, Jacksonville, Florida, USA • **María Aparecida Capellari**, SENAC, São Paulo, Brazil • **Eunice Carrillo Ramos**, Colegio Durango, Naucalpan, Mexico • **Janette Carvalhinho de Oliveira**, Centro de Linguas (UFES), Vitória, Brazil • **María Amelia Carvalho Fonseca**, Centro Cultural Brasil-Estados Unidos, Belém, Brazil • **Audy Castañeda**, Instituto Pedagógico de Caracas, Caracas, Venezuela • **Ching-Fen Chang**, National Chiao Tung University, Hsinchu, Taiwan • **Ying-Yu Chen**, Chinese Culture University, Taipei, Taiwan • **Joyce Chin**, The Language Training and Testing Center, Taipei, Taiwan • **Eun Cho**, Pagoda Language School, Seoul, Korea • **Hyungzung Cho**, MBC Language Institute, Seoul, Korea • **Dong Sua Choi**, MBC Language Institute, Seoul, Korea • **Jeong Mi Choi**, Freelancer, Seoul, Korea • **Peter Chun**, Pagoda Language School, Seoul, Korea • **Eduardo Corbo**, Legacy ELT, Salto, Uruguay • **Marie Cosgrove**, Surugadai University, Saitama, Japan • **María Antonieta Covarrubias Souza**, Centro Escolar Akela, Mexico City, Mexico • **Katy Cox**, Casa Thomas Jefferson, Brasilia, Brazil • **Michael Donovan**, Gakushuin University, Tokyo, Japan • **Stewart Dorward**, Shumei Eiko High School, Saitama, Japan • **Ney Eric Espina**, Centro Venezolano Americano del Zulia, Maracaibo, Venezuela • **Edith Espino**, Centro Especializado de Lenguas - Universidad Tecnológica de Panamá, El Dorado, Panama • **Allen P. Fermon**, Instituto Brasil-Estados Unidos, Ceará, Brazil • **Simão Ferreira Banha**, Phil Young's English School, Curitiba, Brazil • **María Elena Flores Lara**, Colegio Mercedes, Mexico City, Mexico • **Valesca Fróis Nassif**, Associação Cultural Brasil-Estados Unidos, Salvador, Brazil • **José Fuentes**, Empire Language Consulting, Caracas, Venezuela • **José Luis Guerrero**, Colegio Cristóbal Colón, Mexico City, Mexico • **Claudia Patricia Gutiérrez**, Centro Colombo Americano, Cali, Colombia • **Valerie Hansford**, Asia University, Tokyo, Japan • **Gene Hardstark**, Dotkyo University, Saitama, Japan • **Maiko Hata**, Kansai University, Osaka, Japan • **Susan Elizabeth Haydock Miranda de Araujo**, Centro Cultural Brasil Estados Unidos, Belém, Brazil • **Gabriela Herrera**, Fundametal, Valencia, Venezuela • **Sandy Ho**, GEOS International, New York, New York, USA • **Yuri Hosoda**, Showa Women's University, Tokyo, Japan • **Hsiao-I Hou**, Shu-Te University, Kaohsiung County, Taiwan • **Kuei-ping Hsu**, National Tsing Hua University, Hsinchu, Taiwan • **Chia-yu Huang**, National Tsing Hua University, Hsinchu, Taiwan • **Caroline C. Hwang**, National Taipei University of Science and Technology, Taipei, Taiwan • **Diana Jones**, Angloamericano, Mexico City, Mexico • **Eunjeong Kim**, Freelancer, Seoul, Korea • **Julian Charles King**, Qatar Petroleum, Doha, Qatar • **Bruce Lee**, CIE: Foreign Language Institute, Seoul, Korea • **Myunghee Lee**, MBC Language Institute, Seoul, Korea • **Naidnapa Leoprasertkul**, Language Development Center, Mahasarakham University, Mahasarakham, Thailand • **Eleanor S. Leu**, Souchow University, Taipei, Taiwan • **Eliza Liu**, Chinese Culture University, Taipei, Taiwan • **Carlos Lizárraga**, Angloamericano, Mexico City, Mexico • **Philippe Loussarevian**, Keio University Shonan Fujisawa High School, Kanagawa, Japan • **Jonathan Lynch**, Azabu University, Tokyo, Japan • **Thomas Mach**, Konan University, Hyogo, Japan • **Lilian Mandel Civatti**, Associação Cultural Brasil-Estados Unidos, Salvador, Brazil • **Hakan Mansuroglu**, Zoni Language Center, West New York, New Jersey, USA • **Martha McGaughey**, Language Training Institute, Englewood Cliffs, New Jersey, USA • **David Mendoza Plascencia**, Instituto Internacional de Idiomas, Naucalpan, Mexico • **Theresa Mezo**, Interamerican University, Río Piedras, Puerto Rico • **Luz Adriana Montenegro Silva**, Colegio CAFAM, Bogotá, Colombia • **Magali de Moraes Menti**, Instituto Lingua, Porto Alegre, Brazil • **Massoud Moslehpour**, The Overseas Chinese Institute of Technology, Taichung, Taiwan • **Jennifer Nam**, IKE, Seoul, Korea • **Marcos Norelle F. Victor**, Instituto Brasil-Estados Unidos, Ceará, Brazil • **Luz María Olvera**, Instituto Juventud del Estado de México, Naucalpan, Mexico • **Roxana Orrego Ramírez**, Universidad Diego Portales, Santiago, Chile • **Ming-Jong Pan**, National Central University, Jhongli City, Taiwan • **Sandy Park**, Topia Language School, Seoul, Korea • **Patrícia Elizabeth Peres Martins**, Instituto Brasil-Estados Unidos, Rio de Janeiro, Brazil • **Rodrigo Peza**, Passport Language Centers, Bogotá, Colombia • **William Porter**, Osaka Institute of Technology, Osaka, Japan • **Caleb Prichard**, Kwansei Gakuin University, Hyogo, Japan • **Mirna Quintero**, Instituto Pedagógico de Caracas, Caracas, Venezuela • **Roberto Rabbini**, Seigakuin University, Saitama, Japan • **Terri Rapoport**, Berkeley College, White Plains, New York, USA • **Yvette Rieser**, Centro Electrónico de Idiomas, Maracaibo, Venezuela • **Orlando Rodríguez**, New English Teaching School, Paysandu, Uruguay • **Mayra Rosario**, Pontificia Universidad Católica Madre y Maestra, Santiago, Dominican Republic • **Peter Scout**, Sakura no Seibo Junior College, Fukushima, Japan • **Jungyeon Shim**, EG School, Seoul, Korea • **Keum Ok Song**, MBC Language Institute, Seoul, Korea • **Assistant Professor Dr. Reongrudee Soonthornmanee**, Chulalongkorn University Language Institute, Bangkok, Thailand • **Claudia Stanisclause**, The Language College, Maracay, Venezuela • **Tom Suh**, The Princeton Review, Seoul, Korea • **Phiphawin Suphawat**, KhonKaen University, KhonKaen, Thailand • **Craig Sweet**, Poole Gakuin Junior and Senior High Schools, Osaka, Japan • **Yi-nien Josephine Twu**, National Tsing Hua University, Hsinchu, Taiwan • **Maria Christina Uchôa Close**, Instituto Cultural Brasil-Estados Unidos, São José dos Campos, Brazil • **Luz Vanegas Lopera**, Lexicom The Place For Learning English, Medellín, Colombia • **Julieta Vasconcelos García**, Centro Escolar del Lago, A.C., Mexico City, Mexico • **Carol Vaughan**, Kanto Kokusai High School, Tokyo, Japan • **Patricia Celia Veciño**, Instituto Cultural Argentino Norteamericano, Buenos Aires, Argentina • **Isabela Villas Boas**, Casa Thomas Jefferson, Brasilia, Brazil • **Iole Vitti**, Peanuts English School, Poços de Caldas, Brazil • **Gabi Witthaus**, Qatar Petroleum, Doha, Qatar • **Yi-Ling Wu**, Shih Chien University, Taipei, Taiwan • **Chad Wynne**, Osaka Keizai University, Osaka, Japan • **Belkis Yanes**, Freelance Instructor, Caracas, Venezuela • **I-Chieh Yang**, Chung-kuo Institute of Technology, Taipei, Taiwan • **Emil Ysona**, Instituto Cultural Dominico-Americano, Santo Domingo, Dominican Republic • **Chi-fang Yu**, Soo Chow University, Taipei, Taiwan, • **Shigeki Yusa**, Sendai Shirayuri Women's College, Sendai, Japan

To the Teacher

What is *Top Notch*?

- *Top Notch* is a six-level communicative English course for adults and young adults, with two beginning entry levels.
- *Top Notch* prepares students to interact successfully and confidently with both native and non-native speakers of English.
- *Top Notch* demonstrably brings students to a "Top Notch" level of communicative competence.

Key Elements of the *Top Notch* Instructional Design

Concise two-page lessons

Each easy-to-teach two-page lesson is designed for one class session and begins with a clearly stated communication goal and ends with controlled or free communication practice. Each lesson provides vocabulary, grammar, and social language contextualized in all four skills, keeping the pace of a class session lively and varied.

Daily confirmation of progress

Adult and young adult students need to observe and confirm their own progress. In *Top Notch*, students conclude each class session with a controlled or free practice activity that demonstrates their ability to use new vocabulary, grammar, and social language. This motivates and keeps students eager to continue their study of English and builds their pride in being able to speak accurately, fluently, and authentically.

Real language

Carefully exposing students to authentic, natural English, both receptively and productively, is a necessary component of building understanding and expression. All conversation models feature the language people really use; nowhere to be found is "textbook English" written merely to exemplify grammar.

Practical content

In addition to classic topical vocabulary, grammar, and conversation, *Top Notch* includes systematic practice of highly practical language, such as: how to leave and take a phone message, how to request services at a hotel, how to make excuses to decline food you don't like, how to recommend a better deal—usable language today's students want and need.

Memorable model conversations

Effective language instruction must make language memorable. The full range of social and functional communicative needs is presented through practical model conversations that are intensively practiced and manipulated, first within a guided model and then in freer and more personalized formats.

High-impact vocabulary syllabus

In order to ensure students' solid acquisition of vocabulary essential for communication, *Top Notch* contains explicit presentation, practice, and systematic extended recycling of words, collocations, and expressions appropriate at each level of study. The extensive captioned illustrations, photos, definitions, examples, and contextualized sentences remove doubts about meaning and provide a permanent in-book reference for student test preparation. An added benefit is that teachers don't have to search for pictures to bring to class and don't have to resort to translating vocabulary into the students' native language.

Learner-supportive grammar

Grammar is approached explicitly and cognitively, through form, meaning, and use—both within the Student's Book units and in a bound-in Grammar Booster. Charts provide examples and paradigms enhanced by simple usage notes at students' level of comprehension. This takes the guesswork out of meaning, makes lesson preparation easier for teachers, and provides students with comprehensible charts for permanent reference and test preparation. All presentations of grammar are followed by exercises to ensure adequate practice.

English as an international language

Top Notch prepares students for interaction with both native and non-native speakers of English, both linguistically and culturally. English is treated as an international language, rather than the language of a particular country or region. In addition, *Top Notch* helps students develop a cultural fluency by creating an awareness of the varied rules across cultures for: politeness, greetings and introductions, appropriateness of dress in different settings, conversation do's and taboos, table manners, and other similar issues.

Two beginning-level texts

Beginning students can be placed either in *Top Notch 1* or *Top Notch Fundamentals*, depending on ability and background. Even absolute beginners can start with confidence in *Top Notch Fundamentals*. False beginners can begin with *Top Notch 1*. The *Top Notch Placement Test* clarifies the best placement within the series.

Estimated teaching time

Each level of *Top Notch* is designed for 60 to 90 instructional hours and contains a full range of supplementary components and enrichment devices to tailor the course to individual needs.

Components of *Top Notch 2*

Student's Book with Take-Home Super CD-ROM

The Super CD-ROM includes a variety of exciting interactive activities: Speaking Practice, Interactive Workbook, Games and Puzzles, and *Top Notch Pop* Karaoke. The disk can also be played on an audio CD player to listen to the Conversation Models and the *Top Notch Pop* songs.

Teacher's Edition and Lesson Planner

Complete yet concise lesson plans are provided for each class. Corpus notes provide essential information from the *Longman Spoken American Corpus* and the *Longman Learner's Corpus*. In addition, a free *Teacher's Resource Disk* offers the following printable extension activities to personalize your teaching style:

* Grammar self-checks
* *Top Notch Pop* song activities
* Writing process worksheets
* Learning strategies
* Pronunciation activities and supplements
* Extra reading comprehension activities
* Vocabulary cards and cumulative vocabulary activities
* Graphic organizers
* Pair work cards

Copy & Go: Ready-made Interactive Activities for Busy Teachers

Interactive games, puzzles, and other practice activities in convenient photocopiable form support the Student's Book content and provide a welcome change of pace.

Complete Classroom Audio Program

The audio program contains listening comprehension activities, rhythm and intonation practice, and targeted pronunciation activities that focus on accurate and comprehensible pronunciation.

Because *Top Notch* prepares students for international communication, a variety of native *and* non-native speakers are included to ready students for the world outside the classroom. The audio program also includes the five *Top Notch Pop* songs in standard and karaoke form.

Workbook

A tightly linked illustrated Workbook contains exercises that provide additional practice and reinforcement of language concepts and skills from *Top Notch* and its Grammar Booster.

Complete Assessment Package with *ExamView*® Software

Ten easy-to-administer and easy-to-score unit achievement tests assess listening, vocabulary, grammar, social language, reading, and writing. Two review tests, one mid-book and one end-of-book, provide additional cumulative assessment. Two speaking tests assess progress in speaking. In addition to the photocopiable achievement tests, *ExamView*® software enables teachers to tailor-make tests to best meet their needs by combining items in any way they wish.

Top Notch TV

A lively and entertaining video offers a TV-style situation comedy that reintroduces language from each *Top Notch* unit, plus authentic unrehearsed interviews with English speakers from around the world and authentic karaoke. Packaged with the video are activity worksheets and a booklet with teaching suggestions and complete video scripts.

Companion Website

A Companion Website at www.longman.com/topnotch provides numerous additional resources for students and teachers. This no-cost, high-benefit feature includes opportunities for further practice of language and content from the *Top Notch* Student's Book.

Welcome to Top Notch!

About the Authors

Joan Saslow

Joan Saslow has taught English as a Foreign Language and English as a Second Language to adults and young adults in both South America and the United States. She taught English and French at the Binational Centers of Valparaíso and Viña del Mar, Chile, and the Catholic University of Valparaíso. In the United States, Ms. Saslow taught English as a Foreign Language to Japanese university students at Marymount College and to international students in Westchester Community College's intensive English program as well as workplace English at the General Motors auto assembly plant in Tarrytown, NY.

Ms. Saslow is the series director of Longman's popular five-level adult series *True Colors: An EFL Course for Real Communication* and of *True Voices*, a five-level video course. She is author of *Ready to Go: Language, Lifeskills, and Civics*, a four-level adult ESL series; *Workplace Plus*, a vocational English series; and of *Literacy Plus*, a two-level series that teaches literacy, English, and culture to adult pre-literate students. She is also author of *English in Context: Reading Comprehension for Science and Technology*, a three-level series for English for special purposes. In addition, Ms. Saslow has been an author, an editor of language teaching materials, a teacher-trainer, and a frequent speaker at gatherings of EFL and ESL teachers for over thirty years.

Allen Ascher

Allen Ascher has been a teacher and teacher-trainer in both China and the United States, as well as an administrator and a publisher. Mr. Ascher specialized in teaching listening and speaking to students at the Beijing Second Foreign Language Institute, to hotel workers at a major international hotel in China, and to Japanese students from Chubu University studying English at Ohio University. In New York, Mr. Ascher taught students of all language backgrounds and abilities at the City University of New York, and he trained teachers in the TESOL Certificate Program at the New School. He was also the academic director of the International English Language Institute at Hunter College.

Mr. Ascher has provided lively workshops for EFL teachers throughout Asia, Latin America, Europe, and the Middle East. He is author of the popular *Think about Editing: A Grammar Editing Guide for ESL Writers*. As a publisher, Mr. Ascher played a key role in the creation of some of the most widely used materials for adults, including: *True Colors, NorthStar, Focus on Grammar, Global Links*, and *Ready to Go*. Mr. Ascher has an M.A. in Applied Linguistics from Ohio University.

UNIT GOALS

1 Make an excuse to decline food
2 Talk about food passions
3 Discuss lifestyle changes
4 Describe unique foods

A ▸ **TOPIC PREVIEW. Look at the Healthy-Eating Pyramid that suggests daily eating habits to avoid heart disease. Is there anything in the pyramid that you <u>never</u> eat?**

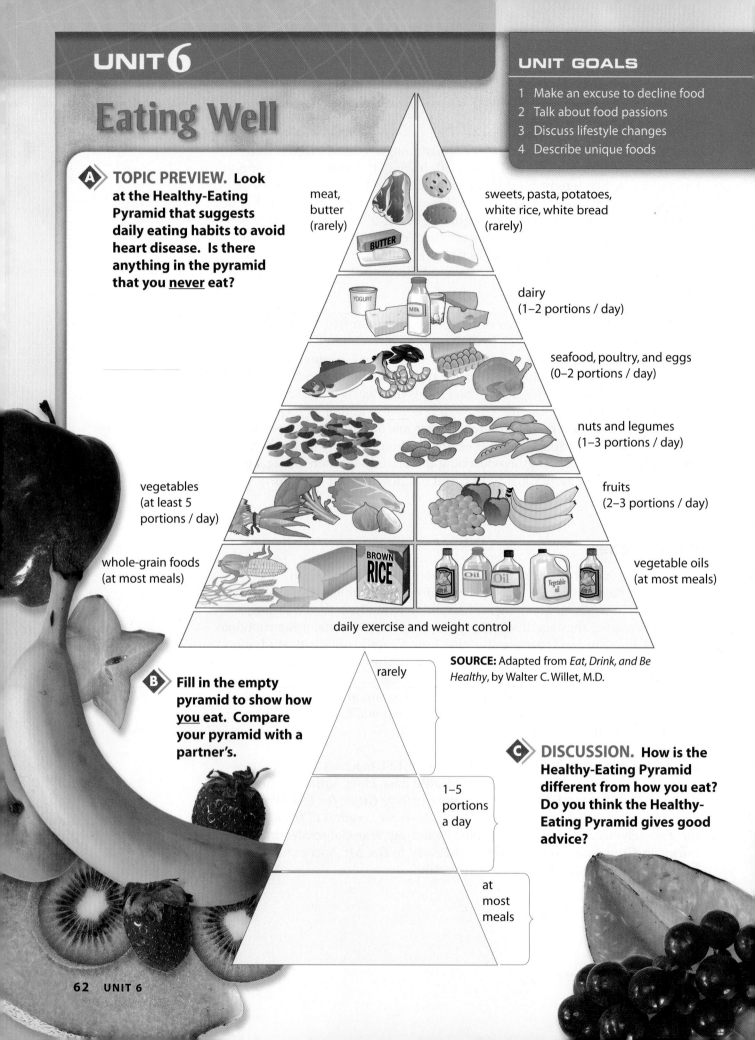

meat, butter (rarely)

BUTTER

sweets, pasta, potatoes, white rice, white bread (rarely)

dairy (1–2 portions / day)

YOGURT

Milk

seafood, poultry, and eggs (0–2 portions / day)

nuts and legumes (1–3 portions / day)

vegetables (at least 5 portions / day)

fruits (2–3 portions / day)

whole-grain foods (at most meals)

BROWN RICE

Oil   Oil   Vegetable oil

vegetable oils (at most meals)

daily exercise and weight control

SOURCE: Adapted from *Eat, Drink, and Be Healthy*, by Walter C. Willet, M.D.

B ▸ **Fill in the empty pyramid to show how <u>you</u> eat. Compare your pyramid with a partner's.**

rarely

1–5 portions a day

at most meals

C ▸ **DISCUSSION. How is the Healthy-Eating Pyramid different from how you eat? Do you think the Healthy-Eating Pyramid gives good advice?**

D 🎧 **SOUND BITES. Read along silently as you listen to a natural conversation.**

IRIS: What in the world are you eating?
TERRI: Chocolate cake. But don't tell anyone, OK?
IRIS: But aren't you on a diet?
TERRI: I used to be. Not anymore.
IRIS: What happened?
TERRI: To tell you the truth, it was just too much trouble.

TERRI: Want to try some?
IRIS: Well, I would. But I'm on a diet.
TERRI: You? I don't believe it! Don't you always have dessert?
IRIS: I used to. Not anymore.
TERRI: Are you sure? You only live once!

E **Check the statements that are true, according to the conversation. Explain your answers.**

- ☐ **1.** Iris doesn't eat sweets now.
- ☐ **2.** Terri doesn't eat sweets now.
- ☐ **3.** Iris doesn't want any cake.
- ☐ **4.** Terri doesn't want any cake.
- ☐ **5.** Iris changed her eating habits.
- ☐ **6.** Terri changed her eating habits.

WHAT ABOUT **YOU?**

Make a list of foods you can eat if ...

you're trying to lose weight.
you're trying to gain weight.

1 *Make an Excuse to Decline Food*

🎧 CONVERSATION **MODEL** Read and listen.

A: Everything's ready. Why don't we sit down?
B: This food looks great!
C: It really smells delicious.

• • •

A: Please help yourself.
C: Thanks. But I'll pass on the chicken.
A: Don't you eat chicken?
C: Actually, no. I'm a vegetarian.
A: I'm sorry. I didn't know that.
C: Don't worry about it. It's not a problem.

🎧 **Rhythm and intonation practice**

A 🎧 **VOCABULARY. Excuses for not eating something. Listen and practice.**

I **don't care for** broccoli.

Coffee **doesn't agree with me**.

I'm **a vegetarian**.

I'm **on a diet**. / I'm **trying to lose weight**.

I'm **avoiding** sugar.

I'm **allergic to** chocolate.

B 🎧 **LISTENING COMPREHENSION. Listen carefully to each conversation. Write the letter to complete each statement. Then listen again to check your work.**

_____ **1.** Cindy
_____ **2.** Frankie
_____ **3.** Marie
_____ **4.** Susan
_____ **5.** George

a. is a vegetarian.
b. is avoiding salt and oil.
c. is trying to lose weight.
d. is allergic to strawberries.
e. doesn't care for fish.

C **GRAMMAR.** Negative <u>yes</u> / <u>no</u> questions and <u>Why don't</u>...?

Use negative <u>yes</u> / <u>no</u> questions ...

• **to check information you think is true.**

| **Isn't** Jane a vegetarian? | Yes, she is. |
| **Don't** they have two sons? | No, they don't. They have three. |

• **when you want someone to agree with you.**

| **Don't** you love Italian food? | Yes. It's delicious. |
| **Wasn't** that a terrible dinner? | Actually, I disagree. I liked it. |

• **to express surprise.**

| **Aren't** you going to have cake? | I'm sorry. I'm on a diet. |
| **Hasn't** he finished eating yet? | I know. Kevin's a very slow eater. |

Use statements with <u>Why don't</u> ...? to make an offer or a suggestion.

| **Why don't** you have some more cake? | Thanks. |
| **Why don't** we go out to eat? | Good idea. |

GRAMMAR BOOSTER

PAGES G10–G11
For more ...

D **Complete each negative <u>yes</u> / <u>no</u> question.**

1. **A:** _____ you allergic to seafood?

   B: Me? No. You're thinking of my brother.

2. **A:** _____ you like your salad?

   B: Not really. It was too spicy for me.

3. **A:** _____ that dinner last night delicious?

   B: It was fantastic!

4. **A:** _____ you already made roast chicken this week?

   B: Yes. Don't you like it?

CONVERSATION
PAIR WORK

Role-play a dinner with friends. Use the pictures and make excuses to decline food.

A: Why don't you help yourself?
B: Thanks. But I'll pass on _____.
A: Don't you _____?
B: _____ ...

Continue the conversation in your <u>own</u> way.

DISCUSSION. Are there any foods you won't eat? Why not?

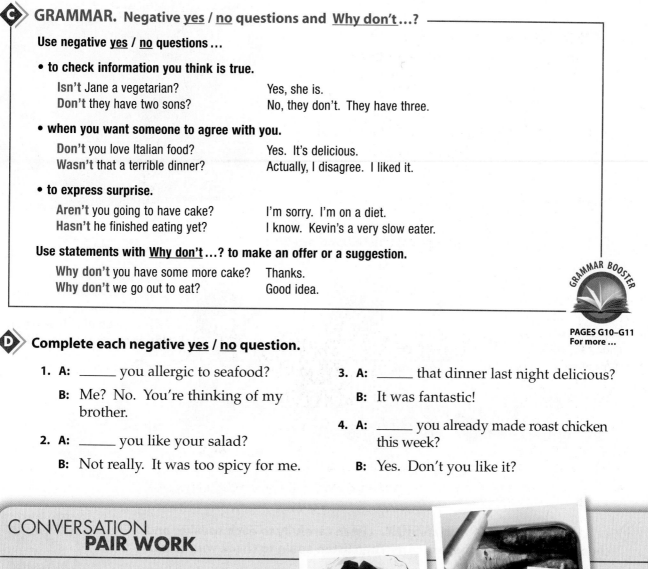

sardines

chocolates

shellfish

tofu

steak

noodles

fries

2 Talk about Food Passions

LESSON

∩ CONVERSATION
MODEL Read and listen.

A: Have you tried the coffee? It's terrific!
B: No, thanks. Are you a big coffee drinker?
A: Definitely. I'm crazy about coffee. What about you?
B: I used to have it a lot. But I've been cutting back.
A: Well, I couldn't live without it.

∩ **Rhythm and intonation practice**

A ∩ **VOCABULARY. Food passions. Listen and practice.**

I'm **crazy about** seafood!
I'm **a big** meat **eater**.
I'm **a big** coffee **drinker**.
I'm **a chocolate addict**.
I'm **a pizza lover**.

I **can't stand** fish!
I'm **not crazy about** chocolate.
I **don't care for** steak.
I'm **not much of a** pizza **eater**.
I'm **not much of a** coffee **drinker**.

B ∩ **LISTENING COMPREHENSION. Listen carefully to each speaker and check the statements that are true. Then listen again to check your work.**

1. a. ☐ She's crazy about sushi.   b. ☐ She can't stand sushi.
2. a. ☐ He's not crazy about asparagus.   b. ☐ He loves asparagus.
3. a. ☐ She's a mango lover.   b. ☐ She doesn't care for mangoes.
4. a. ☐ He's a big pasta eater.   b. ☐ He isn't crazy about pasta.
5. a. ☐ She can't stand ice cream.   b. ☐ She's an ice cream addict.

sushi

asparagus

mangoes

pasta

ice cream

C **PAIR WORK. Use the vocabulary to tell your partner about <u>your</u> food passions.**

D GRAMMAR. Used to

Use <u>used to</u> and the base form of a verb for habitual actions in the past that are not true now.

My daughter **used to love** candy. But now she doesn't care for it.

I **didn't use to eat** vegetables. But now I'm crazy about them.

Questions and answers

Didn't Mary **use to avoid** sweets?   Yes, she did. / No, she didn't.

What did you **use to eat** for breakfast?   Eggs and sausage. But not anymore.

GRAMMAR BOOSTER

PAGE G12
For more ...

E 🎧 PRONUNCIATION. <u>Used to</u>. Notice how /tu/ often reduces to /tə/ in <u>used to</u>. Listen and repeat.

1. I used to eat fatty foods.

2. Jack used to like sweets.

3. Sally used to be a vegetarian.

4. I used to like seafood.

F Complete each sentence logically with <u>used to</u> or <u>didn't use to</u>.

1. Tom _____ eat a lot of fatty foods. But now he avoids them.

2. Carol _____ hate fish. But now she's crazy about it.

3. Arthur _____ have vegetables. But now he has them all the time.

4. Victor _____ drink a lot of coffee. But now he doesn't care for it very much.

5. Nancy _____ eat many sweets. But now she does.

6. Fran _____ go out to restaurants a lot. But now she eats at home more often.

G PAIR WORK. Ask your partner questions about things he or she used to do but doesn't do now.

CONVERSATION
PAIR WORK

Complete the chart with foods you like and dislike. Then role-play a dinner party conversation about food passions with a partner. Use the guide, or create a new conversation.

A: Have you tried the _____? _____ terrific!

B: No, thanks. Are you _____?

A: _____. What about you?

B: _____ ...

Continue the conversation in your <u>own</u> way.

Foods I'm crazy about	Foods I can't stand

CONTROLLED PRACTICE

3 Discuss Lifestyle Changes

A ▶ **READING WARM-UP.** Do you think people's eating habits are better or worse than they used to be?

B 🎧 **READING.** Read the article. Use the glossary for new words.

Changing Lifestyles Contribute to Obesity

Seth Mydans, *The New York Times*

Around the world, more than one billion adults are overweight, and at least 300 million of these are classified as obese. While this used to be a problem primarily in the West, the number of obese Asians has been increasing dramatically. Obesity is spreading throughout Asia, especially among children, as people move to big cities, where they eat fattier fast foods and live a more sedentary lifestyle.

"We spoil him," says Warisa Waid, a teacher in Bangkok, Thailand, of her 11-year-old son, Saharat. "We don't care if it is good or bad; we just feed him whatever he wants." She adds, "He spends most of his time in front of the TV, playing video games and watching cartoons."

When Saharat was younger, he was small for his age. "His father's family believes that being skinny is bad, so they kept telling me, 'Why don't you feed your kid more?' and, 'What's wrong with him?' His grandparents give him fast food, pizza, and all that." She adds, "He loves deep-fried stuff, and he doesn't eat vegetables at all."

In Asian cities, processed foods and fast foods rich with sugar and saturated fats are often the most available and the cheapest. At the same time, people are getting less physical exercise. Dr. Augusto D. Litonjua of the Philippines blames what he calls "malling," which he defines as spending the day in shopping malls and eating at fast-food restaurants.

Milk, ice cream, cookies, soft drinks, and potato chips—once all foreign foods—are as common in many parts of Asia now as in the West. People are eating more meat and eggs and less rice and vegetables. In the last two decades, Thais have doubled their annual intake of sugar.

The World Health Organization (WHO) reports that 6 out of 10 deaths in the region are due to diseases that may be linked to obesity—heart attacks, stroke, diabetes, hypertension, and some forms of cancer.

GLOSSARY
sedentary not active

processed foods foods that are not fresh; e.g., frozen or canned

heart attack sudden damage to the heart because the blood flow is blocked

stroke damage caused when an artery in the brain stops working

diabetes a disease in which there is too much sugar in the blood

hypertension high blood pressure

cancer a disease which produces a growth that can cause death

SOURCE: Adapted by permission from *The New York Times*

C Check the statements that are true, according to the article. Explain your answers.

☐ **1.** Obesity is a new health problem in Asia.

☐ **2.** Saharat Waid is on a diet now.

☐ **3.** Many Asians are going to exercise classes in malls.

☐ **4.** Asians are eating foods today that they didn't use to eat.

☐ **5.** Obesity is not a serious problem.

D **DISCUSSION.**

1. How are people's lifestyles in your city similar to those described in the article? How are they different?

2. What advice would you give Warisa Waid?

TOP NOTCH
INTERACTION • *Changing lifestyles*

STEP 1. GROUP WORK. Complete the class survey and discuss the results.

Lifestyle Survey

1. How many students have ever tried some kind of a diet to lose weight? What diets have they tried?

No. of students _____

Examples
- ☐ ate less food
- ☐ avoided desserts
- ☐ avoided fatty foods
- ☐ other _____
_____

2. How many students have changed the way they eat to avoid illness? How?

No. of students _____

Examples
- ☐ don't eat sugar
- ☐ don't eat fast foods
- ☐ eat whole grains
- ☐ other _____
_____

3. How many students lead an active, non-sedentary lifestyle? What do they do?

No. of students _____

Examples
- ☐ work out in a gym
- ☐ play sports
- ☐ walk or run
- ☐ other _____
_____

Total number of students in the class ☐

STEP 2. PAIR WORK. On your notepad, write some positive and negative lifestyle changes you have made in your life. Then compare your notes with a partner's. Talk about how your eating and exercise habits have changed in your life.

> ❝I didn't use to go to a gym, but now I do. That was a positive change.❞

Some positive changes	Some negative changes

STEP 3. DISCUSSION. How have most people's eating and exercise habits changed over the last 20 years?

> ❝People are eating a lot more fast foods. I don't think that's a good thing.❞

STEP 4. WRITING. Write about how people's lifestyles have changed for the better or worse.

4 *Describe Unique Foods*

A 🎧 VOCABULARY. Food descriptions. Listen and practice.

It looks terrific.

It smells terrible.

It tastes
{ sweet.
spicy.
salty.
sour. }

It smells like
It tastes like
It looks like
} chicken.

It's { soft.
hard. }

It's { chewy.
crunchy. }

B 🎧 LISTENING COMPREHENSION. First, listen to descriptions of foods from around the world and write the letter of each food. Then listen again and use the vocabulary to complete each description.

☐ **1.** It's _chewy_, and it tastes _sweet_.

☐ **2.** It tastes _____, and it's _____.

☐ **3.** It's _____, and it tastes _____.

☐ **4.** It tastes _____. Some think it looks _____.

☐ **5.** It tastes _____, and it smells _____.

☐ **6.** They're _____, and they're _____.

a kim chee / Korea cabbage

b chapulines / Mexico grasshopper

c mochi / Japan

d Vegemite® / Australia

e Jell-O® / United States

f cho dofu / China

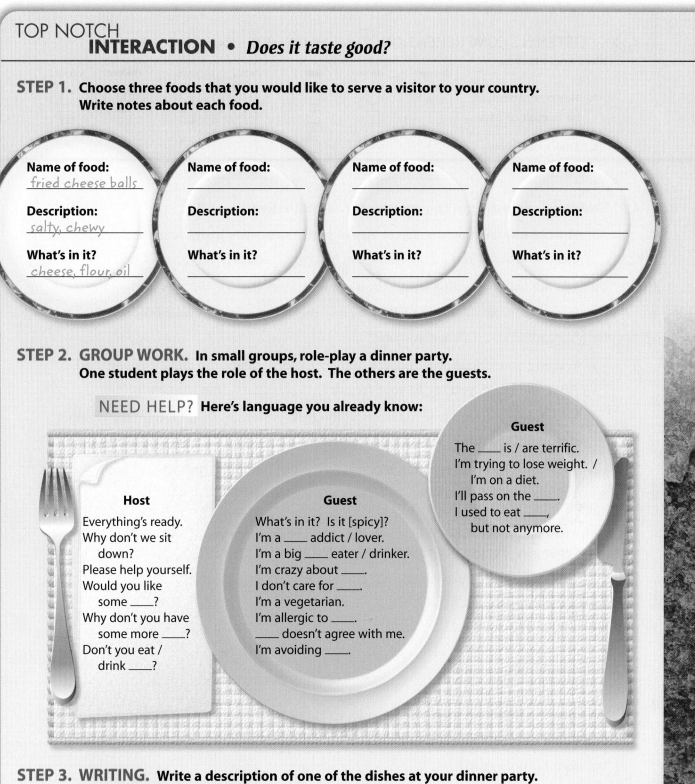

INTERACTION • *Does it taste good?*

STEP 1. Choose three foods that you would like to serve a visitor to your country. Write notes about each food.

Name of food:
fried cheese balls

Description:
salty, chewy

What's in it?
cheese, flour, oil

Name of food:
_____

Description:
_____

What's in it?
_____

Name of food:
_____

Description:
_____

What's in it?
_____

Name of food:
_____

Description:
_____

What's in it?
_____

STEP 2. GROUP WORK. In small groups, role-play a dinner party. One student plays the role of the host. The others are the guests.

NEED HELP? **Here's language you already know:**

Guest
The ____ is / are terrific.
I'm trying to lose weight. /
    I'm on a diet.
I'll pass on the ____.
I used to eat ____,
    but not anymore.

Host

Everything's ready.
Why don't we sit
    down?
Please help yourself.
Would you like
    some ____?
Why don't you have
    some more ____?
Don't you eat /
    drink ____?

Guest

What's in it? Is it [spicy]?
I'm a ____ addict / lover.
I'm a big ____ eater / drinker.
I'm crazy about ____.
I don't care for ____.
I'm a vegetarian.
I'm allergic to ____.
____ doesn't agree with me.
I'm avoiding ____.

STEP 3. WRITING. Write a description of one of the dishes at your dinner party. Use the questions as a guide.

Is it an appetizer? An entrée? A dessert?

When do people eat it? Every day? On holidays?

When was the first time you tried it?

CHECKPOINT

A **LISTENING COMPREHENSION. Listen and check the foods that each person likes and dislikes.**

	shrimp	clams	fish	steak	pasta	chicken	carrots
1. He's crazy about...	☐	☐	☐	☐	☐	☐	☐
He doesn't care for...	☐	☐	☐	☐	☐	☐	☐
2. She's crazy about...	☐	☐	☐	☐	☐	☐	☐
She doesn't care for...	☐	☐	☐	☐	☐	☐	☐

B **Complete a negative <u>yes</u> / <u>no</u> question for each situation.**

1. You see a woman on the street. You're pretty sure she's Joan Chen, the famous Chinese actress. You go up to her and ask her: "_Aren't you_ Joan Chen?"

2. You are walking with a friend. You're pretty sure you see Michael Jordan, the famous basketball player, walking across the street. You ask your friend: "_____ Michael Jordan?"

3. You and your friend went out for dinner. Unfortunately, the meal was very bad. After you leave, you say to your friend: "_____ the food awful?"

4. You and your friend enjoyed a day at the park yesterday. You thought the weather was really beautiful. You say to your friend: "_____ the weather beautiful?"

5. Your new classmate is eating lunch at 3:00 p.m. You are surprised because it's so late. You say to your classmate: "_____ lunch yet?"

C **Write five sentences about things you did or didn't do when you were younger. Use <u>used to</u> or <u>didn't use to</u>.**

1. _____.
2. _____.
3. _____.
4. _____.
5. _____.

D **Describe the following foods in your <u>own</u> way.**

Example: carrots _They're orange and they're sweet and crunchy_.

1. squid (or octopus) _____.
2. ice cream _____.
3. bananas _____.
4. cabbage _____.
5. steak _____.

TOP NOTCH **PROJECT**
Find articles about food and health in your local newspapers or magazines. Discuss them with your class.

TOP NOTCH **WEBSITE**
For Unit 6 online activities, visit the *Top Notch* Companion Website at www.longman.com/topnotch.

UNIT WRAP-UP

- **Grammar.** Write five negative <u>yes</u> / <u>no</u> questions.
  Doesn't the chicken look delicious?

- **Social language.** Look at the dishes and the ingredients. Then role-play conversations with a partner about the food.

International Buffet
TODAY'S SELECTIONS

"Caramel Apple" / United States

Ingredients:
apples, butter, brown sugar, nuts

"Beef and Broccoli" / China

Ingredients:
beef, red peppers, peanut oil, garlic, broccoli, onions, mushrooms

"Rain Doughnuts" / Brazil

Ingredients:
flour, milk, eggs, sugar, oil

"Bi Bim Bop" / Korea

Ingredients:
rice, beef, soy sauce, sesame oil, garlic, black pepper, salt, eggs, lettuce, rice wine, hot pepper sauce

"Pad Thai" / Thailand

Ingredients:
rice noodles, chicken, tofu, peanuts, fish sauce, sugar, lime juice, vegetable oil, garlic, shrimp, eggs, hot peppers

"Arepas" / Venezuela

Ingredients:
corn flour, salt, white cheese, oil

"Chicken Mole" / Mexico

Ingredients:
chicken, salt, vegetable oil, onions, garlic, tomatoes, chocolate

---

✔ Now I can ...

- ☐ make an excuse to decline food.
- ☐ talk about food passions.
- ☐ discuss lifestyle changes.
- ☐ describe unique foods.

Psychology and Personality

UNIT GOALS
1 Discuss color preferences
2 Cheer someone up
3 Determine your personality type
4 Discuss the impact of birth order on personality

A **TOPIC PREVIEW.** Is color important to you? Do colors have meanings? Take the color survey.

1. tomato red	2. berry red	3. deep red	4. red-purple	5. mauve	6. pink	7. fuchsia
8. purple	9. light purple	10. blue-purple	11. blue	12. medium light blue	13. light blue	14. dark blue
15. blue-green	16. deep blue-green	17. green	18. emerald green	19. lime green	20. light green	21. dark green
22. dark yellow-green	23. muted yellow-green	24. yellow-green	25. yellow	26. dark yellow	27. yellow-orange	28. light yellow
29. orange	30. pink-orange	31. light orange	32. brown	33. orange-brown	34. golden brown	35. light brown
36. white	37. cream	38. black	39. dark gray	40. gray	41. blue-gray	
42. silver	43. platinum	44. gold				

Please let us know what you think about color! Eight easy questions! There are no wrong answers. Use the color chart. You can use the same color more than once!

1 Which is your **favorite** color? _____

2 Which is your **least favorite** color? _____

3 Which color do you associate with **happiness**? _____

4 Which color do you associate with **purity**? _____

5 Which color do you associate with **good luck**? _____

6 Which color do you associate with **death**? _____

7 Which color do you associate with **power**? _____

8 Which color or color combinations are **bad luck**? _____

SOURCE: Adapted from the Color Matters® Global Color Survey http://express.colorcom.com

B **DISCUSSION.** Where do you think color preferences come from: our culture or our own individual tastes?

🎧 **SOUND BITES.** Read along silently as you listen to a natural conversation.

TRACY: So what do you feel like doing after dinner?
SARAH: I don't know. You decide. I'm kind of down in the dumps.

TRACY: You do look a little blue. Something wrong?
SARAH: Nothing I can put my finger on. I guess I'm just feeling a little out of sorts since I got back from vacation.
TRACY: Maybe a nice dinner will cheer you up.

D **UNDERSTAND MEANING FROM CONTEXT.** **Complete each statement, according to the conversation.**

1. When Sarah says she's "kind of down in the dumps," she means _____.
   a. She's feeling sad.   b. She's feeling happy.

2. When Tracy tells Sarah she looks "a little blue," she means _____.
   a. Sarah looks sad.   b. Sarah looks happy.

3. When Sarah says she's feeling "a little out of sorts," she means _____.
   a. She's feeling sad.   b. She's feeling happy.

E **PAIR WORK.** **Answer the questions together.**

1. What's Sarah's problem?
2. What does Tracy suggest?

WHAT ABOUT **YOU?**

Answer each question. Then compare your answers with a partner's.

1. What makes you feel blue? _____

2. What cheers you up when you're down in the dumps? _____

3. What do you do to help a friend who's feeling down? _____

1 ▶ *Discuss Color Preferences*

🎧 CONVERSATION MODEL Read and listen.

A: You know, I'd like to repaint the kitchen.
B: OK. What color?
A: How about gray?
B: Well, I don't mind repainting it, but gray's out of the question.
A: Why? What's wrong with gray?
B: It's boring.
A: Really? To me, gray's calm, not boring.

🎧 **Rhythm and intonation practice**

A **GRAMMAR.** Gervnds and infinitives after certain verbs

> **Gerund:** an -*ing* form of a verb (*painting*)
>
> **Infinitive:** <u>to</u> + a base form (*to paint*)

Gerunds

She enjoys **painting**.

They discussed **going** on vacation.

Infinitives

He wants **to paint** the bedroom red.

I decided **to exercise** more often.

Use a gerund after the following verbs: avoid, can't stand, discuss, dislike, enjoy, feel like, (don't) mind, practice, quit, suggest.

Use an infinitive after the following verbs: agree, be sure, choose, decide, expect, hope, learn, need, plan, seem, want, wish, would like.

GRAMMAR BOOSTER

PAGES G13–G14
For more …

B Complete the advice for the "blues." Use gerunds and infinitives.

Learn to be your own best friend!

Everybody feels a little blue from time to time. · If you _____
                  1. not feel like / talk

about it and you _____ advice books, here are some helpful
           2. dislike / read

hints. First of all, _____ your health. _____ coffee
       3. decide / take care of   4. Avoid / drink

and alcohol. Exercise can be very helpful. If you _____, I
                  5. choose / exercise

_____ with a friend you _____ with. _____
  6. suggest / go   7. enjoy / laugh   8. Be sure / eat

right and, importantly, _____ lots of sleep. If you _____
         9. be sure / get   10. would like / take

a day off from work and you _____ to the movies or
         11. want / go

_____ a walk in the park, just do it. _____ yourself
  12. plan / take   13. Learn / cheer

up. You can be your own best friend! Oh, and a final note: Everybody finds

certain colors "happy." Try to wear the colors <u>you</u> find most cheerful.

C 🎧 **PRONUNCIATION.** Reduction of <u>to</u> in infinitive phrases. **Notice how unstressed <u>to</u> reduces to /tə/. Listen and repeat.**

1. I decided to repaint the bedroom.
2. She needs to get lots of sleep.

3. We plan to drive downtown tomorrow.
4. I know you'd like to travel more.

D 🎧 **VOCABULARY.** Adjectives of emotion. **Listen and practice.**

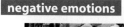

a **happy** event   an **exciting** game   a **cheerful** scene   a **calm** child

negative emotions

a **sad** occasion   a **depressing** day   a **disgusting** scene   a **nervous** person

E 🎧 **LISTENING COMPREHENSION.** Listen to the conversations. **Then complete each statement with the color and the adjective of emotion.**

1. He thinks _____ is a _____ color.
2. She thinks the _____ suit will be _____.
3. He thinks the _____ chair will make him _____.
4. She doesn't like _____ shoes. She thinks they're _____.

CONVERSATION
PAIR WORK

Discuss repainting a room or buying a new car, new clothes, shoes, or something else. Compare tastes in color. Use the guide, or create a new conversation.

A: You know, I'd like to _____.
B: _____. What color?
A: How about _____?
B: _____ …

Continue the conversation in your <u>own</u> way.

CONTROLLED PRACTICE

2 Cheer Someone Up

🎧 CONVERSATION MODEL Read and listen.

A: You look down. What's up?

B: Oh, nothing serious. I'm just tired of the same old grind. But thanks for asking.

A: I know what you mean. I'm tired of working, too. How about going to a movie?

B: Great idea. Let's go!

🎧 **Rhythm and intonation practice**

Ⓐ GRAMMAR. Gerunds after prepositions

You can use a gerund as the object of a preposition.

	preposition	object
We can go to a movie instead	**of**	**watching** TV.
Thanks	**for**	**asking**.
They believe	**in**	**being** honest.

Don't use an infinitive as the object of a preposition.

(NOT We can go to a movie instead of ~~to watch TV~~.)

adjective + preposition

angry about	
excited about	afraid of
happy / sad about	sick / tired of
	bored with

verb + preposition

complain about	
talk about	apologize for
worry about	believe in
	object to

GRAMMAR BOOSTER

PAGE G14
For more ...

Ⓑ Complete the descriptions of Ted and Nicole with prepositions and gerunds.

Have I ever told you about my childhood? Well, I was a terrible student!

Ted is an extrovert. Like most extroverts, he's direct. And he's honest; he believes _____ the truth.
1. tell

At his job, he works with other people and he never complains _____ long
2. work

hours. He doesn't worry _____ work on weekends
3. have to

or holidays.

He has a few fears, though. Most of all, he's afraid _____.
4. fly

Ted's wife, Nicole, on the other hand, is an introvert. But she doesn't object _____ about herself from time to time.
5. talk

Right now, she's bored _____ a student, and she's sick and tired _____ so many long reports and _____ exams every few weeks! She's angry _____ spend so much time in front of a computer.
6. be
7. write
8. take
9. have to

But she's excited _____ on vacation. Unlike Ted, she's not at all afraid _____!
10. go
11. fly

C PAIR WORK. Fill out the form for yourself, using gerunds. Then share information with a partner.

" Right now, I'm happy about getting engaged! "

Right now, what are you . . .

happy about? _____

excited about? _____

bored with? _____

sick and tired of? _____

CONVERSATION
PAIR WORK

Role-play cheering someone up. Use the guide and suggestions, or create a new conversation.

A: You look _____. What's up?

B: Oh, nothing serious. I'm just tired of _____. But thanks for asking.

A: I know what you mean. _____.

B: _____.

💡 **Suggestions . . .**

- Why don't we [go for a walk]?
- Maybe a [vacation] would cheer you up.
- Would you like me to [make you some soup]?
- How about some [ice cream]? That always makes me feel better!
- Your own suggestion

CONTROLLED PRACTICE

3 *Determine Your Personality Type*

A 🎧 **LISTENING COMPREHENSION. Listen to the discussion between a professor and his students. What's the subject of the conversation?**

B 🎧 **Listen again and check the statements that are true, according to the professor.**

☐ **1.** Not everyone has a personality.

☐ **2.** A person's personality includes the usual behavior, thoughts, and emotions of that person.

☐ **3.** Emotions and thoughts are the same thing.

☐ **4.** The word "emotion" is similar in meaning to the word "feeling."

☐ **5.** The people in a family almost always have similar personalities.

☐ **6.** Personality comes only from the environment.

C **Match each word with an explanation from the discussion. Listen again, if necessary, to check your answers.**

_____ **1.** personality

_____ **2.** thoughts

_____ **3.** emotions

_____ **4.** genetics

_____ **5.** the environment

_____ **6.** nature

_____ **7.** nurture

a. everything you learn from: family, culture, and life experiences

b. another word for genetics in discussing personality

c. traits that come from the parents

d. feelings, such as love, anger, fear, and hate

e. a person's pattern or style of behavior

f. memories, wishes, and plans

g. another word for environment in discussing personality

D **DISCUSSION. Where do you think you got your personality—more from "nature" or more from "nurture"?**

TOP NOTCH
INTERACTION • *Introvert or extrovert?*

STEP 1. Determine your personality type. Find out if you are an introvert or an extrovert by completing the following survey.

ARE YOU AN INTROVERT OR AN EXTROVERT?

Instructions: From each pair of personality traits, check one that sounds like <u>your</u> personality. At the end, add up your selections for each column. Then decide for yourself: Are you an introvert or an extrovert?

Extroverts tend to:	Introverts tend to:
1. ○ enjoy being in a group.	○ enjoy being alone.
2. ○ need to interact with others.	○ avoid interacting unnecessarily.
3. ○ be active.	○ be quiet.
4. ○ be interested in events.	○ be interested in feelings.
5. ○ sometimes talk without thinking.	○ usually think without talking.
6. ○ be easy to "understand."	○ be hard to know.
7. ○ know many people a little.	○ know few people, but well.
8. ○ talk.	○ listen.
9. ○ seek excitement.	○ seek peace.
10. ○ say what they mean.	○ keep their ideas to themselves.

Total extrovert selections ○   Total introvert selections ○

○ I'm an extrovert.   ○ I'm an introvert.   ○ I'm a mixture of both!

SOURCE: Excerpted and adapted from "Discover your personality type" www.win.net

STEP 2. GROUP WORK. Talk about the personality traits you checked. Find a real example from your life to explain.

> " I'm an extrovert. I like to sing for people and act in plays. "

STEP 3. WRITING. Write about your own personality. Talk about your personality traits. Explain whether you are an introvert or an extrovert. Give examples and reasons.

> I'm an extrovert, just like my father. I am talkative, open and honest, and I dislike being alone. I have a lot of friends, and I love going out with them in a large group...

4 ▶ Discuss the Impact of Birth Order on Personality

A ▶ **READING WARM-UP.** Do you think the first child in a family has different personality traits from children who are born later?

B ▶ 🎧 **READING.** Read the article. Which description sounds like **your** personality?

When did you arrive in your family? Are you the oldest child, a middle child, or the "baby"? Birth order may not be the _most_ important factor in personality development, but we can make some generalizations.

If you're the OLDEST, you're probably:

- successful.
- conservative.
- self-critical—always feeling you could do better.
- able to enjoy the company of older people.

Parents often expect a lot from the first child. They often push them to succeed. The first child often has to grow up very fast.

If you're a MIDDLE child, you're probably:

- the one with the most friends.
- the silent rebel against the family's values.

Middle children often feel less important than their older or younger siblings.

If you're the YOUNGEST child, you're probably:

- a show-off who enjoys the limelight.
- often the family clown, making everyone laugh.
- both charming and a rebel—lovable one minute and breaking rules the next.
- creative in art, music, and other ways.

The youngest child often has the longest childhood.

SOURCE: Theresa M. Campbell www.suite101.com

C ▶ **Find these words in the article. Then complete each statement with one of the words.**

clown
values
self-critical
creative
charming
rebel
sibling

1. Another word for a brother or a sister is a _____.
2. The cultural rules within each family are its _____.
3. Another word for lovable is _____.
4. People who feel they should "do better" are _____.
5. A person who doesn't follow the rules is a _____.
6. Artists, musical composers, and writers are _____.
7. A person who enjoys making other people laugh is a _____.

D ▶ **DISCUSSION.** In families you know, are the descriptions in the article generally true? Give examples to support your opinion.

INTERACTION • *First child, middle child, or youngest child?*

STEP 1. **Fill out the checklist for yourself.**

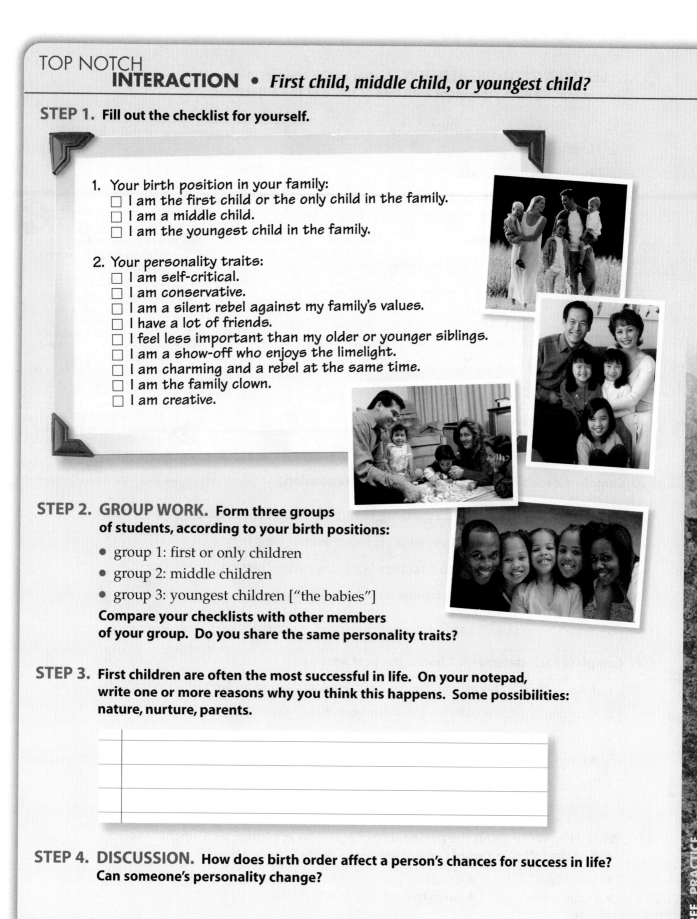

1. Your birth position in your family:
   - ☐ I am the first child or the only child in the family.
   - ☐ I am a middle child.
   - ☐ I am the youngest child in the family.

2. Your personality traits:
   - ☐ I am self-critical.
   - ☐ I am conservative.
   - ☐ I am a silent rebel against my family's values.
   - ☐ I have a lot of friends.
   - ☐ I feel less important than my older or younger siblings.
   - ☐ I am a show-off who enjoys the limelight.
   - ☐ I am charming and a rebel at the same time.
   - ☐ I am the family clown.
   - ☐ I am creative.

STEP 2. GROUP WORK. Form three groups of students, according to your birth positions:

- group 1: first or only children
- group 2: middle children
- group 3: youngest children ["the babies"]

Compare your checklists with other members of your group. Do you share the same personality traits?

STEP 3. First children are often the most successful in life. On your notepad, write one or more reasons why you think this happens. Some possibilities: nature, nurture, parents.

STEP 4. DISCUSSION. How does birth order affect a person's chances for success in life? Can someone's personality change?

FREE PRACTICE

A 🎧 **LISTENING COMPREHENSION. Listen to the conversations. Then complete each statement with one or more of the adjectives.**

1. She prefers _____ music.
2. He finds the weather _____.
3. She's expecting her vacation to be _____.
4. She thinks white is _____.

happy	sad
exciting	depressing
cheerful	boring
calm	disgusting

B Write your <u>own</u> response.

1. "I'm feeling really down in the dumps."
   YOU _____.

2. "Anything I can do?"
   YOU _____.

3. "She's tired of the same old grind."
   YOU _____.

4. "What's wrong?"
   YOU _____.

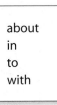

🎧 *TOP NOTCH SONG*
"The Colors of Love"
Lyrics on last page before Workbook.

TOP NOTCH PROJECT
Make a list of well-known people you consider very successful. Find information about the size of their families and where each person was in the birth order of his or her family.

TOP NOTCH WEBSITE
For Unit 7 online activities, visit the *Top Notch* Companion Website at www.longman.com/topnotch.

C Complete each statement with the correct preposition.

   Extroverts don't worry _____ talking in public. They believe _____
   _{1.}   _{2.}
   being honest, and they get bored _____ being alone. They may
                                    _{3.}
   talk _____ staying home and reading a book, but when they do,
       _{4.}
   they complain _____ having no one to talk to. They object _____
                 _{5.}   _{6.}
   being by themselves.

about
in
to
with

D Complete each statement. Choose the best answer.

1. John is such an (extrovert / introvert). He loves being around other people.
2. Our usual pattern of behavior is our (genetics / personality).
3. Another word for characteristics is (nurture / traits).
4. Many people believe that (self-criticism / birth order) affects personality development.
5. The nature-nurture controversy is an argument about the origin of the (environment / personality).

E **WRITING. Write about the personality of a person you know well. Include some or all of the following words and expressions in your description.**

- self-critical
- conservative
- creative
- an extrovert
- an introvert
- a clown
- a rebel

UNIT WRAP-UP

- **Narration.** Tell a story, using the pictures.
- **Social language.** Create conversations for the wife and husband.
- **Writing.** Write about the family at the beach. Describe the personalities of the children.

✔ Now I can ...

- ☐ discuss color preferences.
- ☐ cheer someone up.
- ☐ determine my personality type.
- ☐ discuss the impact of birth order on personality.

85

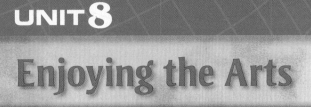

UNIT 8

Enjoying the Arts

UNIT GOALS

1 Recommend a museum
2 Describe an object
3 Talk about how art fits in your life
4 Discuss your favorite artists

A TOPIC PREVIEW. Which of these pieces of art have you seen before? Are you familiar with the artists?

The Great Wave of Kanagawa / print (woodcut)
artist: Katsushika Hokusai, Japan (around 1830)

Dutch Interior I / oil painting
artist: Joan Miró, Spain (1928)

36 1/8" x 28 3/4". Mrs. Simon Guggenheim Fund.
(163.1945). ©2004 Successio Miro/Artist Rights
Society ARS, NY. The Museum of Modern Art/
Licensed by Scala-Art Resource, NY.

White Flower on Red Earth, #1 / oil painting
artist: Georgia O'Keeffe, U.S.A. (1943)

The Grinder / oil painting
artist: Diego Rivera, Mexico (1926)

Rivera, Diego (1886-1957). The Grinder (La molendera).
1926. Oil on cavas, 35 7/16 x 46 1/16 in. Museo Nacional de
Arte Moderno, Instituto Nacional de Bellas Artes, Mexico City,
D.F., Mexico. (c) Banco de Mexico Diego Rivera & Frida Kahlo
Museums Trust. Av. Cinco de Mayo No. 2, Col. Centro, Del.
Cuauhtemoc 06059, Mexico, D.F. Reproduction authorized by
the Instituto Nacional de Bellas Artes y Literatura. Courtesy of
Art Resource. NY.

B Which of these pieces of art do you like the best? Why?

> ❝I love the Georgia O'Keeffe. I love nature, and the colors of the painting are very exciting.❞

C 🎧 **SOUND BITES.** **Read along silently as you listen to a natural conversation.**

JOE: This print's sort of interesting. It says it was painted in 1903. I kind of like it.
EMMA: Is it a Picasso?
JOE: Yes, it is. It would look nice over my desk.
EMMA: Don't you find it a little too dark?
JOE: No. I think it's just right.

EMMA: Hey, what about this Warhol? What do you think?
JOE: I don't know. I'm not really too crazy about his stuff.
EMMA: Just look at the colors!
JOE: I guess I'm not into really bright colors. I prefer the Picasso.
EMMA: To each his own.

D **Classify the statements. Check the ones that indicate likes. Write an "X" for the ones that indicate dislikes.**

☐ **1.** This print's sort of interesting.
☐ **2.** I kind of like it.
☐ **3.** Don't you find it a little too dark?

☐ **4.** I think it's just right.
☐ **5.** I'm not really too crazy about his stuff.
☐ **6.** I'm not into really bright colors.

WHAT ABOUT **YOU?**

What kinds of art do you prefer?

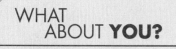

☐ painting   ☐ drawing   ☐ photography   ☐ sculpture

☐ fashion   ☐ film   ☐ pottery   ☐ other _____

1 Recommend a Museum

⌒ CONVERSATION MODEL Read and listen.

A: Be sure not to miss the Prado Museum while you're in Madrid.

B: Really? Why's that?

A: Well, for one thing, *Las Meninas* is kept there.

B: No kidding! I've always wanted to see that.

A: They have a great collection of paintings. You'll love it.

B: Thanks for the suggestion!

⌒ **Rhythm and intonation practice**

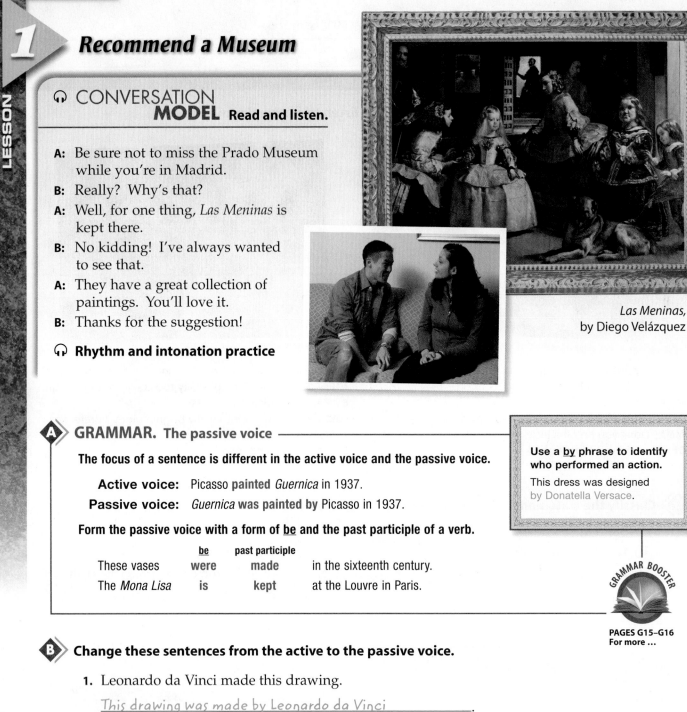

Las Meninas,
by Diego Velázquez

A GRAMMAR. The passive voice

The focus of a sentence is different in the active voice and the passive voice.

> **Active voice:** Picasso **painted** *Guernica* in 1937.
> **Passive voice:** *Guernica* **was painted by** Picasso in 1937.

Form the passive voice with a form of <u>be</u> and the past participle of a verb.

	be	**past participle**	
These vases	were	made	in the sixteenth century.
The *Mona Lisa*	is	kept	at the Louvre in Paris.

> Use a <u>by</u> phrase to identify who performed an action.
>
> This dress was designed by Donatella Versace.

GRAMMAR BOOSTER

PAGES G15–G16
For more ...

B Change these sentences from the active to the passive voice.

1. Leonardo da Vinci made this drawing.

   This drawing was made by Leonardo da Vinci _____.

2. Imogen Cunningham took that photograph in 1903.

   _____.

3. Vincent Van Gogh painted *The Starry Night* in 1889.

   _____.

4. Federico Fellini directed the film *La Strada* in 1954.

   _____.

5. Katsushika Hokusai made that print over a century ago.

   _____.

1. No **KIDD**ing!
2. You'll **LOVE** it!

3. That's **PER**fect!
4. How **IN**teresting!

CONVERSATION
PAIR WORK

Recommend a museum. Use the guide and the pictures, or create a new conversation about museums you know.

A: Be sure not to miss _____ while you're in _____.
B: Really? Why's that?
A: Well, for one thing, _____ is kept there.
B: _____.
A: They have a great collection of _____.
B: _____.

The National Palace Museum / Taipei, Taiwan

Known for its huge collection of Chinese painting, pottery, sculpture, and crafts.

Travelers Among Mountains and Streams, by Fan K'uan

David, by Michelangelo

The Accademia Gallery / Florence, Italy

Six million visitors a year! Famous for its collection of sculptures by Michelangelo!

The Louvre Museum / Paris, France

The world's largest art museum! And some of the world's greatest art!

Mona Lisa, by Leonardo da Vinci

CONTROLLED PRACTICE

89

2 *Describe an Object*

🎧 CONVERSATION
MODEL Read and listen.

A: Excuse me. What's this figure made of?
B: Wood. It's handmade.
A: Really? Where was it made?
B: Mexico. What do you think of it?
A: It's <u>fantastic</u>.

🎧 **Rhythm and intonation practice**

🎧 **positive adjectives**
fantastic
gorgeous
wonderful
cool (very informal)

A 🎧 **VOCABULARY.** Materials. **Listen and practice.**

glass   silver   gold   clay   wood   stone   cloth

B **PAIR WORK.** **Point to one of the objects. Ask and answer questions about materials.**

❝What's the English chair made of?❞

❝It's made of wood.❞

▲ an English chair

▲ an Egyptian figure

▲ an Italian vase

▲ a Mexican bowl

▲ a Spanish bag

▲ a Japanese figure

C ▷ GRAMMAR. The passive voice: questions

Yes / no questions

Were these wood bowls **made** in Africa?   Yes, they were. / No, they weren't.

Was this stone figure **carved** by the Incas?   Yes, it was. / No, it wasn't.

Information questions

Where **were** these cloth figures **made**?   In Brazil.

When **was** this picture **painted**?   It was painted in the 1960s.

What **are** these clay bowls **used** for?   They're used for cooking.

How **was** it **made**?   All by hand.

GRAMMAR BOOSTER

PAGE G17
For more …

D ▷ Unscramble the words to write questions.

1. were / Where / carved / those / wood figures _____?

2. made / were / those /dolls / How _____?

3. Was / painted / that / clay bowl / by hand _____?

4. was / taken / When / that / photograph _____?

E ▷ Write an information question for each statement.

1. *How were the glass figures made* ?   The glass figures were made by hand.

2. _____?   The pottery is used for carrying water.

3. _____?   The gold figure was made hundreds of years ago.

4. _____?   The wood chairs were built in Venezuela.

5. _____?   The bowl was made by machine.

CONVERSATION
PAIR WORK

☺ It's / They're	fantastic. / gorgeous. / wonderful. / cool.
☹ I'm not crazy about / I don't care for	it. / them.
It's / They're	not for me.

Discuss the art objects. Use the guide, or create a new conversation.

A: What _____ made of?

B: _____.

A: Really? Where _____ made?

B: _____. What do you think of _____?

A: _____ …

Continue the conversation in your own way.

◀ dolls from Guatemala

◀ a vase from Korea

◀ a figure from Peru

◀ a vase from France

◀ a figure from Peru

◀ a figure from New Zealand

CONTROLLED PRACTICE

3 ▷ Talk about How Art Fits in Your Life

A▷ **READING WARM-UP.** Is art an important part of your life?
Do you think artistic talent is genetic?

B▷ 🎧 **READING.** *Top Notch* interviewed two people about the role of art in their lives.

LIVING WITH ART

Yu Gan's son, Kuai (above)

Yu Gan's father, (left)

I n 1982, Lynn Contrucci bought a beautiful piece of jewelry from Mali, in West Africa. She liked the piece so much that she began to study African art in order to understand it better. She was selling her house at the time, and she had some money to spend—so she started to collect African art. Since then, it has become a passion. She has collected nearly 300 pieces, including figures and masks. "I'm an addict now! My family thinks I'm crazy," she jokes. Even her windows and bed are decorated with beautiful African cloth. Some pieces are given as gifts to family and friends, or they are sold just to make room for more. In 1998, she began to get interested in Chinese jade figures and Tibetan paintings. More recently, she began collecting Haitian paintings. "My home is a mixture of art from all these places," she says.

Ms. Contrucci says it is like bringing people into her home. "Each piece has a special meaning. They are my friends."

Y u Gan is an artist from a family of talented artists. He began painting at the age of seven and never stopped. His father, Yu Heng, is known internationally for his dramatic traditional paintings, calligraphy, and poetry. His brother, Yu Ping, is a sculptor and painter. His sister, Yu Fan, is both a pianist and an artist. His wife, Yan Liu, is a fashion design artist, and his son, Kuai—who has shown strong artistic talent since the age of three—wants to be a filmmaker.

Mr. Yu paints in an abstract style that combines, as he puts it, "the best traditions of Western and Eastern art." Like traditional Chinese artists, he is inspired by images from nature—earth and water. Like Western artists, he works with oil paint to express his feelings. He hopes to influence young Chinese with his art. "Today, they turn away from all things Chinese and love all things Western. I want them to understand that they can take the best from both worlds." Mr. Yu has a website at www.eChinaArt.com, which was created to promote art by Chinese artists worldwide.

"I am totally captivated by art," says Mr. Yu. "I can't imagine life without it."

SOURCE: Authentic *Top Notch* interviews

C ▷ DISCUSSION.

1. Why does Lynn Contrucci's family think she's crazy? Do <u>you</u> think she is?

2. What does Yu Gan mean when he says, "I am totally captivated by art"? Are <u>you</u>?

3. Which best describes you? Explain your answer.

    a. I collect art.   **b.** I make art.   **c.** I appreciate art.   **d.** I don't care about art.

TOP NOTCH
INTERACTION • *Is art important in your life?*

STEP 1. PAIR WORK. Answer the questions with a partner. Explain each answer.

1. Do you or does anyone in your family have artistic talent?
2. Do you have any friends with artistic talent?
3. How often do you visit art museums or galleries?
4. Do you decorate your home with art objects?

STEP 2. On your notepad, write notes about some art that decorates your home.

piece	notes
wood figure	made in Santos/small, has bright colors/helps me remember my vacation

piece	notes

STEP 3. GROUP WORK. Tell your class about the art that decorates your home. Use your notepad for support.

NEED HELP? **Here's language you already know:**

Questions

What [is it] used for?
Where [are they] from?
When [was it] made?
How [were they] made?

Likes and dislikes

I'm into ____.
I'm crazy about ____.
I don't care for____.
I can't stand ____.
I prefer ____.

Descriptions

[They're] called ["worry beads"].
[It's] made of [wood].
[They were] made by [children].

93

FREE PRACTICE

4 ▸ Discuss Your Favorite Artists

A ▸ 🎧 VOCABULARY. How to describe influences. Listen and practice.

be inspired by   She **is inspired by** nature. She tries to copy nature's beauty in her paintings.

be influenced by   He **was influenced by** the Mexican muralist Diego Rivera's art. Their paintings often have the same themes.

be interested in   He **has** always **been interested in** men's fashion. He reads about the newest designs in magazines.

be fascinated by   She**'s fascinated by** the films of Ingmar Bergman, the Swedish director. She watches them again and again.

be moved by   She **is** really **moved by** Sebastião Salgado's photographs. His images of children sometimes make her cry.

B ▸ WHAT ABOUT YOU? What are you interested in? Inspired by? Fascinated by?

C ▸ 🎧 LISTENING COMPREHENSION. Listen to the biography of Vincent Van Gogh. In your opinion, did he have an interesting life? Listen again and check T (<u>true</u>) or F (<u>false</u>).

PART 1

T F
□ □ **1.** Van Gogh studied art as a child.

□ □ **2.** In Paris, Van Gogh was influenced by the work of other artists.

□ □ **3.** Van Gogh didn't care for Japanese art.

PART 2

T F
□ □ **4.** In Arles, Van Gogh was inspired by the colors of the French countryside.

□ □ **5.** Before Van Gogh died, his brother came from Paris to be with him.

□ □ **6.** Many of his paintings were sold when he lived in Arles.

Zundert—the small village in Holland where Van Gogh was born

Self-portrait with Cut-off Ear and Bandage, by Van Gogh

The town of Arles in southern France

Vase with Fourteen Sunflowers, by Van Gogh

TOP NOTCH
INTERACTION • *I'm really into Picasso!*

STEP 1. Look at some famous artists. Add your <u>own</u> favorites. Then write notes about your favorite artists on the notepad.

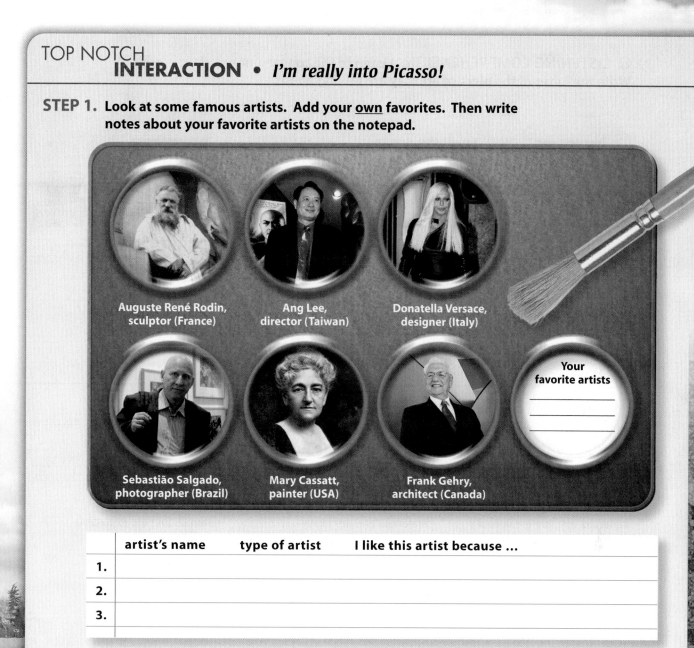

Auguste René Rodin,
sculptor (France)

Ang Lee,
director (Taiwan)

Donatella Versace,
designer (Italy)

Sebastião Salgado,
photographer (Brazil)

Mary Cassatt,
painter (USA)

Frank Gehry,
architect (Canada)

Your favorite artists
_____
_____
_____

	artist's name	type of artist	I like this artist because ...
1.			
2.			
3.			

STEP 2. GROUP WORK. Discuss your favorite artists. Tell your class why you like them.

❝I'm a real fan of Frida Kahlo and Diego Rivera. I'm fascinated by their lives.❞

❝Donatella Versace is my favorite designer. Her fashions are so contemporary!❞

❝I love Ang Lee. His films are very interesting. My favorite is *Crouching Tiger, Hidden Dragon*.❞

95

FREE PRACTICE

CHECKPOINT

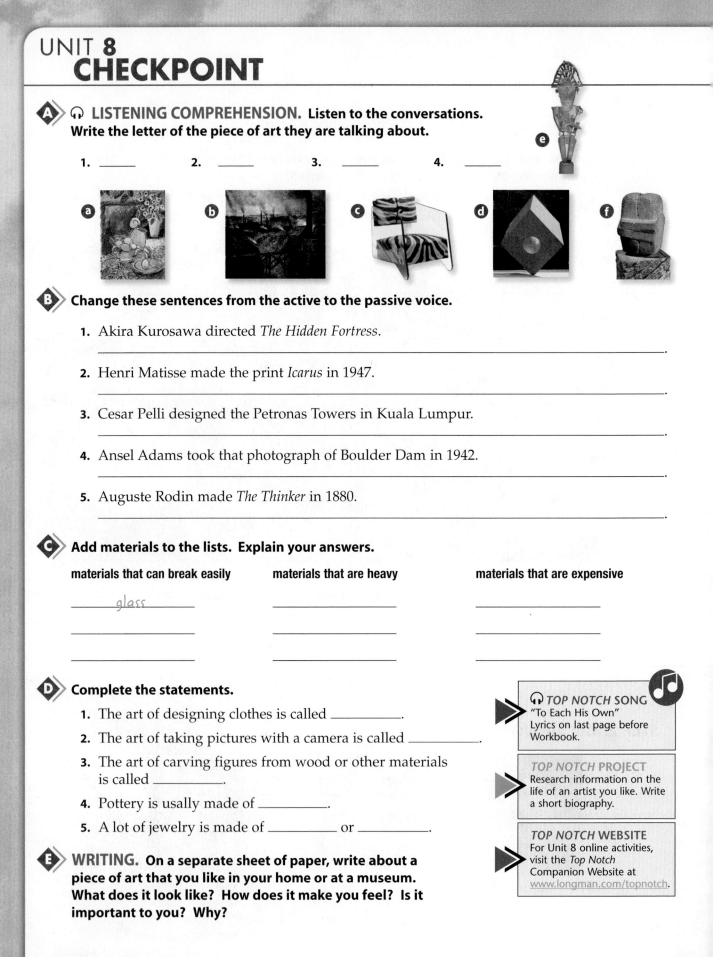

A 🎧 **LISTENING COMPREHENSION. Listen to the conversations. Write the letter of the piece of art they are talking about.**

1. _____   2. _____   3. _____   4. _____

B **Change these sentences from the active to the passive voice.**

1. Akira Kurosawa directed *The Hidden Fortress*.

_____.

2. Henri Matisse made the print *Icarus* in 1947.

_____.

3. Cesar Pelli designed the Petronas Towers in Kuala Lumpur.

_____.

4. Ansel Adams took that photograph of Boulder Dam in 1942.

_____.

5. Auguste Rodin made *The Thinker* in 1880.

_____.

C **Add materials to the lists. Explain your answers.**

materials that can break easily	materials that are heavy	materials that are expensive
glass	_____	_____
_____	_____	_____
_____	_____	_____

D **Complete the statements.**

1. The art of designing clothes is called _____.
2. The art of taking pictures with a camera is called _____.
3. The art of carving figures from wood or other materials is called _____.
4. Pottery is usally made of _____.
5. A lot of jewelry is made of _____ or _____.

E **WRITING. On a separate sheet of paper, write about a piece of art that you like in your home or at a museum. What does it look like? How does it make you feel? Is it important to you? Why?**

🎧 *TOP NOTCH* SONG
"To Each His Own"
Lyrics on last page before Workbook.

TOP NOTCH PROJECT
Research information on the life of an artist you like. Write a short biography.

TOP NOTCH WEBSITE
For Unit 8 online activities, visit the *Top Notch* Companion Website at www.longman.com/topnotch.

UNIT WRAP-UP

- **Discussion.** Talk about the pieces of art you like, and why.
- **Grammar.** Make statements in the passive voice about the art.
- **Social language.** Create conversations for the people.

THE GREAT MUSEUMS OF LONDON

THE NATIONAL GALLERY

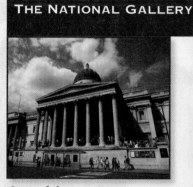

The Arnolfini Marriage, by Jan van Eyck (1434)

One of the greatest collections of European paintings in the world.

THE VICTORIA AND ALBERT MUSEUM

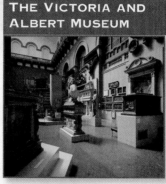

The Luck of Edenhall, Syria, 13th century

The greatest museum of decorative art in the world. A permanent collection of fashion, sculpture, ceramics, glass, silver and jewelry, furniture, photography, and paintings.

THE TATE GALLERY

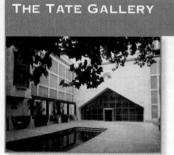

Mustard on White, by Roy Lichtenstein (1963)

The best of British art and a major new gallery of modern art.

THE BRITISH MUSEUM

Discus thrower, Rome, 5th century B.C.E.

Best known for its exhibits of art from ancient Egypt, Greece, and Rome.

✔ *Now I can ...*

- ☐ recommend a museum.
- ☐ describe an object.
- ☐ talk about how art fits in my life.
- ☐ discuss my favorite artists.

Living with Computers

Unit Goals

1 Recommend a better deal
2 Troubleshoot a problem
3 Describe how you use computers
4 Discuss the social impact of the Internet

A **TOPIC PREVIEW.** Look at the electronics store website. Which of these computer accessories do you already have? Which would you like to have?

al.thecoolstuff.com
WHAT THE FUTURE HAS IN STORE FOR YOU!

Shop by Departments
Weekly Specials
Computers
Computer Accessories
Software
Photo
Video
Audio
Appliances
Entertainment

HOME | my order | account | login | view cart | SEARCH [____] GO

CHECK OUT OUR NEW MODELS!

monitors

microphones and headsets

speakers

CD drives

NEED A NEW MOUSE? CHECK OUT OUR PRICES!

keyboards and mice

NEW GAMES AVAILABLE

games and joysticks

CHECK OUT OUR NEW UPDATES!

Adobe Acrobat 5.0
Adobe GoLive 4.0
Microsoft Windows NT Server

software

B **DISCUSSION.** Where do <u>you</u> get the latest information on computer and other electronics products? What are the advantages of shopping for these products online?

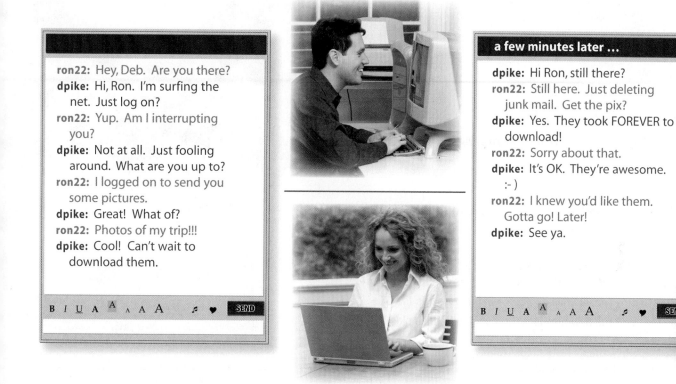

C 🎧 **SOUND BITES.** Read along silently as you listen to an instant message "conversation."

ron22: Hey, Deb. Are you there?
dpike: Hi, Ron. I'm surfing the net. Just log on?
ron22: Yup. Am I interrupting you?
dpike: Not at all. Just fooling around. What are you up to?
ron22: I logged on to send you some pictures.
dpike: Great! What of?
ron22: Photos of my trip!!!
dpike: Cool! Can't wait to download them.

B I U A A A A A ♪ ♥ SEND

a few minutes later ...

dpike: Hi Ron, still there?
ron22: Still here. Just deleting junk mail. Get the pix?
dpike: Yes. They took FOREVER to download!
ron22: Sorry about that.
dpike: It's OK. They're awesome. :-)
ron22: I knew you'd like them. Gotta go! Later!
dpike: See ya.

B I U A A A A A ♪ ♥ SEND

D Deb and Ron shortened sentences in their instant messages.
Complete their statements with the words in the box.

| I'm | Did you | I | See you | They're | Are you |

1. "_____ just log on?"
2. "_____ just fooling around."
3. "_____ photos of my trip!!!"

4. "_____ can't wait to download them."
5. "_____ still there?"
6. "_____ later!"

WHAT ABOUT **YOU?**

Check <u>yes</u>, <u>no,</u> or <u>not sure</u>.

Do you know what to do if:	yes	no	not sure
1. you get an instant message?	☐	☐	☐
2. your printer won't print?	☐	☐	☐
3. you can't get on the Internet?	☐	☐	☐
4. your computer crashes?	☐	☐	☐

1 Recommend a Better Deal

🎧 CONVERSATION MODEL Read and listen.

A: I'm thinking about getting a new monitor.
B: Oh, yeah? What kind?
A: Everyone says I should get a Macro.
B: Well, I've heard that the Panatel is as good as the Macro, but it costs a lot less.
A: Really? I'll check it out.

🎧 **Rhythm and intonation practice**

A ▶ GRAMMAR. Comparisons with <u>as ... as</u>

Similarity

Use <u>as</u> ... <u>as</u> to say that two things are equal or the same.
Use the adverb <u>just</u> for emphasis.

> The F30 has **as many new features as** the LX.
> The new monitor is **just as good as** the old one.

Use the adverb <u>almost</u> to say two things are very similar, but not exactly the same.

> The X20 is **almost as good** as the X15. But it's a little slower.

Difference

Use <u>not as</u> ... <u>as</u> to say that two things are different.
Use the adverb <u>quite</u> when the difference is very small.

> My new air conditioner isn't **as noisy as** the old one.
> The F30 doesn't cost **quite as much as** the LX.

Use the adverb <u>nearly</u> to say that there's a big difference.

> Our old monitor wasn't **nearly as big as** the new one. The new one is much bigger.

Short statements with <u>as</u>

> We loved our old monitor. But our new monitor is **just as good**.
> Have you seen Carol's new car? My car isn't **nearly as nice**.

GRAMMAR BOOSTER

PAGES G17–G18
For more ...

B Read the statements. Write sentences with <u>as ... as</u>. Use the adverbs.

1. The Macro computer game is easy to use. The Spartica computer game is also easy to use.

   (just) _____.

2. The new RCO keyboard is popular. The one from Digitek is popular too.

   (just) _____.

3. The C50 monitor is large. The C30 monitor is a little larger than the C50 monitor.

   (almost) _____.

4. Hampton's new laptop has many new features. Jackson's new laptop also
   has many new features.

   (just) _____.

5. The PBS speakers are powerful. The CCV speakers are much more powerful.

   (not / nearly) _____.

6. The Panex digital camera costs US$330. The RDP digital camera costs US$360.

   (not / quite) _____.

C 🎧 PRONUNCIATION. Stress in <u>as ... as</u> phrases. Listen and repeat.

1. The new laptop is as fast as the old one.

2. The old monitor was just as large as the new one.

3. My new keyboard isn't nearly as nice as the old one.

CONVERSATION
PAIR WORK

Student A: choose a product from *Buyer's Friend Magazine.*
Student B: recommend a better deal from *Electronics Guide Magazine.*

Use the guide, or create a new conversation.

A: I'm thinking about getting a new _____.
B: _____? What kind?
A: Everyone says I should get a _____.
B: Well, I've heard that the _____.
A: Really? I'll check it out.

BUYER'S FRIEND *Magazine*

Our recommendations!

■ Mott Optical Mouse	very good	US$25
■ Mott X16 Keyboard	very comfortable	US$19
■ Mott Super Web Camera	easy to use	US$256
■ Mott Z30 Monitor	17 inches	US$260

Electronics GUIDE magazine

YOUR BEST BUYS!

Rico PF Mouse	very good	US$20
Rico P30 Keyboard	very comfortable	US$15
Rico Ultra Web Camera	easy to use	US$200
Rico PH1 Monitor	20 inches	US$260

CONTROLLED PRACTICE

Troubleshoot a Problem

🎧 CONVERSATION
MODEL Read and listen.

A: Eugene, could you take a look at this?

B: Sure. What's the problem?

A: Well, I clicked on the toolbar to save a file and the computer crashed.

B: Why don't you try restarting? That sometimes works.

A: OK. I'll give that a try.

🎧 **Rhythm and intonation practice**

A 🎧 **VOCABULARY.** Computer commands. **Listen and practice.**

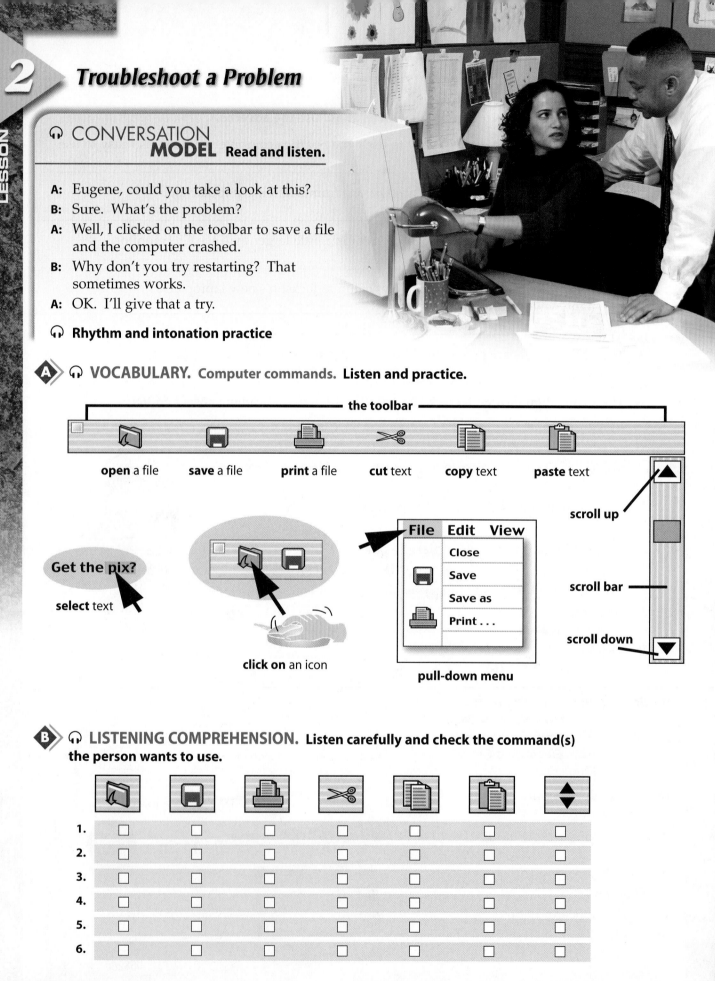

the toolbar

open a file   save a file   print a file   cut text   copy text   paste text

scroll up

Get the pix?

select text

click on an icon

File   Edit   View
Close
Save
Save as
Print . . .

pull-down menu

scroll bar

scroll down

B 🎧 **LISTENING COMPREHENSION.** Listen carefully and check the command(s) the person wants to use.

1.	☐	☐	☐	☐	☐	☐	☐
2.	☐	☐	☐	☐	☐	☐	☐
3.	☐	☐	☐	☐	☐	☐	☐
4.	☐	☐	☐	☐	☐	☐	☐
5.	☐	☐	☐	☐	☐	☐	☐
6.	☐	☐	☐	☐	☐	☐	☐

C ▷ GRAMMAR. The infinitive of purpose

The following two sentences have the same meaning.

I scrolled down **to read** the text. = I scrolled down **because I wanted to read** the text.

Use an infinitive to express a purpose.

I put the cursor on the pull-down menu **to close** the file.

Put the cursor on the toolbar **to choose** a command.

You can use short answers with infinitives to answer questions about purpose.

Why did you click on that icon?   **To save** the file before I close it.

Why did you click on that word?   **To select** it so I can copy it.

PAGES G18–G19
For more …

D ▷ PAIR WORK. Look at Pat's To-Do List. Ask and answer questions. Use the infinitive of purpose.

❝Why is Pat going to talk to her boss?❞ ❝To ask for a vacation day.❞

TO-DO

talk to boss—ask for a vacation day

go to supermarket—buy chicken for lunch with Mom

call Mom—invite her for lunch

take car to garage—get an oil change

meet John—help him shop for a new suit

E ▷ Complete each sentence in your <u>own</u> way. Use infinitives of purpose.

1. You can click on the print icon…
2. Put the cursor on the pull-down menu…
3. I bought a new scanner…
4. I e-mailed my friend…
5. I logged on to the Internet…

CONVERSATION PAIR WORK

Ask for help with a computer problem. Use the guide, or create a new conversation.

A: _____, could you take a look at this?
B: Sure. _____?
A: Well, I _____ and _____.
B: Why don't you _____?
A: _____…

Continue the conversation in your <u>own</u> way.

💡 **Some ideas…**

- The computer crashed.
- The printer won't print.
- The file won't open.
- your own idea

CONTROLLED PRACTICE

3 Describe How You Use Computers

A 🎧 VOCABULARY. Things to do on the Internet. Listen and practice.

1. surf the Internet

2. join a chat room

4. scan pictures

3. send an attachment

5. create a web page

B 🎧 LISTENING COMPREHENSION. Listen to the people talk about how they use their computers. Check each person's activities.

	Dave Grant	Cecilia Rivas	Michael Teoh	Isabelle Dewar
surfs the Internet	☐	☐	☐	☐
sends instant messages	☐	☐	☐	☐
scans pictures	☐	☐	☐	☐
downloads files	☐	☐	☐	☐
has joined a chat room	☐	☐	☐	☐
has created a website	☐	☐	☐	☐
has sent an attachment	☐	☐	☐	☐

INTERACTION • *Are you a computer addict?*

STEP 1. Complete the consumer information card about your <u>own</u> computer use.

1. I use a computer
- ☐ for work.
- ☐ for study.
- ☐ for fun.
- ☐ I never use a computer.

2. I use a computer
- ☐ to surf the Internet.
- ☐ to send instant messages.
- ☐ to keep in touch with people.
- ☐ to download music files.
- ☐ to create websites.
- ☐ to send e-mail.
- ☐ to write reports.
- ☐ to join chat rooms.
- ☐ to download pictures.
- ☐ other _____

FIRST CLASS MAIL
NO POSTAGE
NECESSARY

3. I spend _____ hours a week on a computer.
- ☐ 0–10
- ☐ 11–20
- ☐ 21–30
- ☐ 31–40
- ☐ 41–50
- ☐ over 50

4. Compared to other people I know,
- ☐ I don't spend nearly as much time on a computer as they do.
- ☐ I spend just as much time on a computer as they do.
- ☐ I spend WAY too much time on a computer.
- ☐ you could say I'm a computer addict.

5. ☐ People come to me for help when they have computer trouble. They consider me an expert.

STEP 2. GROUP WORK. Walk around your classroom and ask your classmates questions. Write their names on the chart.

Find someone who ...	Name
1. is a computer expert.	
2. is a computer addict.	
3. is afraid of computers.	
4. uses the Internet to meet new people.	
5. uses the Internet to avoid people.	

STEP 3. Tell your class about your classmates and how they use the computer.

4   Discuss the Social Impact of the Internet

A   **READING WARM-UP.** What kinds of problems have you had with the Internet? What kinds of problems with the Internet have you heard about on the news?

B   🎧 **READING.** Read the articles about some serious problems with the Internet. Which do you think is the most serious?

China Computers Face Virus Epidemic

Four out of five computers in China, the world's largest computer and Internet market, have been affected by computer viruses, according to a report in the official state news service, China Daily. "Only 16 percent of computer users reported they were free from any viruses in their computers," reports researcher, Zhang Jian. Viruses sent through the Internet are destroying information and causing too many computers to crash, the China Daily said.

SOURCE: cnn.com

Another Hacker Hits Microsoft

One week after Microsoft reported that a hacker had gotten into its computer networks, another hacker said he entered the company's web servers on Friday. The hacker, using the name Dimitri, logged on to several of Microsoft's web servers and downloaded files containing confidential company information. A Microsoft spokesperson said, "There is always a possibility that hackers can get into a company's computer network…. There are bad people out there who will try to do bad things."

SOURCE: archive.infoworld.com

Internet Fraud Grows Worldwide

You can buy almost anything online. But did you know you could use the Internet to buy stolen credit card numbers? Internet fraud is a growing international problem. There are people out there who will buy your credit card numbers to purchase things online and have them sent to their homes. "We have people on staff constantly watching this kind of activity all over the world," said Jeff King of CyberSource, a company that manages online billing. "It definitely keeps you very busy."

SOURCE: internetnews.com

Police Look for Internet Predator

Carla White was a popular 13-year-old and a good student. But she was also meeting strangers on the Internet. Last May, Carla was found strangled to death, and police believe she met her killer online. "I can't believe she's dead," said one of her classmates. "How could anyone do this to her?" Police chief Martin Beck warns, "Parents need to know that when their children visit chat rooms, there are Internet predators out there who may want to hurt them."

SOURCE: usatoday.com

Based on the articles, predict the person who would make each of these statements. Explain your answer.

_____ 1. "Kids should be very careful on the Internet. It's very scary."

_____ 2. "Our company needs better ways to protect our files from people outside."

_____ 3. "It's costing our company a lot of time and money to make sure customers are billed correctly."

_____ 4. "There are still too many computers in this country that may crash."

a. Martin Beck, police chief
b. Zhang Jian, researcher
c. Jeff King, CyberSource
d. A Microsoft spokesperson

TOP NOTCH
INTERACTION • *Life in cyberspace*

STEP 1. Read the beginning of an article about the social impact of the Internet.

> Computers have changed people's lives, and in most cases for the better. However, you have to balance the benefits with the problems—for every benefit there is also a bad side. On the good side, information is available to everyone quickly and easily through the Internet. On the bad side, not all information you find on the Internet is true. You have to check carefully before you can believe all that you read.

STEP 2. PAIR WORK. Discuss some of the benefits and problems of computers and the Internet. Talk about your own experiences and things you have heard or read about in the news. Make a list of them on your notepad.

Benefits	Problems
You can meet new people online.	Bad people use the Internet, too.

Benefits	Problems

STEP 3. GROUP WORK. Discuss the benefits and problems of computers and the Internet. Compare notes and write a list of benefits and problems on the board.

STEP 4. WRITING. Write a short article about the social impact of computers and the Internet. Include information about the benefits and problems.

107

FREE PRACTICE

A 🎧 **LISTENING COMPREHENSION. Listen to the conversations. Choose the words that best describe each product. Then listen again to check your answers.**

1. The C40 Monitor is _____ the Z8 Monitor.
   a. the same as   **b.** larger than   **c.** smaller than

2. The Hip Web Camera is _____ the Pentac Web Camera.
   a. the same as   **b.** cheaper than   **c.** more expensive than

3. Mundite's new CD drive is _____ Mundite's old CD drive.
   a. the same as   **b.** faster than   **c.** slower than

4. Play Zone's computer game is _____ New World's game.
   a. the same as   **b.** less fun than   **c.** more fun than

B **Write a response to each statement in your <u>own</u> way.**

1. "Gotta go! Later!"
   (YOU) _____.

2. "I'm thinking about getting a new computer."
   (YOU) _____.

3. "I clicked on save and my computer crashed."
   (YOU) _____.

C **Answer each question in your <u>own</u> way, using an infinitive of purpose.**

1. Why do people join chat rooms? _____.

2. Why do people e-mail their friends? _____.

3. Why do people surf the Internet? _____.

4. Why do people visit electronics store websites? _____.

5. Why are you studying English? _____.

D **Complete the following statements.**

1. If you want to print a document, click on the print _____.

2. To read more text on your screen, use the scroll _____ to scroll down.

3. If you want to see what other things you can do, click on the _____ menu.

4. When you're finished working on a document, don't forget to _____ it before you close the file.

> *TOP NOTCH* **PROJECT**
> Find articles in your local newspapers and magazines about computer or Internet benefits or problems. Tell your class about them.

> *TOP NOTCH* **WEBSITE**
> For Unit 9 online activities, visit the *Top Notch* Companion Website at www.longman.com/topnotch.

E **WRITING. Write about how you use a computer. Talk about how often you use it and what you do with it. Or write about someone you know who uses a computer.**

UNIT WRAP-UP

- **Vocabulary.** Name the computer parts and accessories.
- **Grammar.** Write statements using the infinitive of purpose.
- **Social language.** Create conversations for the people.

Now I can ...

- ☐ recommend a better deal.
- ☐ troubleshoot a problem.
- ☐ describe how people use computers.
- ☐ discuss the social impact of the Internet.

UNIT 10

Ethics and Values

UNIT GOALS

1 Return someone else's property
2 Discuss ethical choices
3 Express personal values
4 Discuss honesty

A **TOPIC PREVIEW.** Study the situations. What do you think each person should do?

B **DISCUSSION.** Have you ever had a similar experience to any of these situations? What did you do?

C 🎧 **SOUND BITES.** **Read along silently as you listen to a natural conversation.**

MATT: I'm going to get a tattoo.
PAUL: Your parents would let you do that?
MATT: Are you kidding? If I asked them, they'd just say no.
PAUL: You mean you're not going to tell them?
MATT: I'd have to be nuts to ask them. But, there's nothing wrong with tattoos. Everybody has them.
PAUL: Maybe … Matt, I hate to say this, but I think you're making a mistake. You should get permission. If you don't, I'm sure you'll be sorry.
MATT: OK. I'll give it some thought.

 D **PAIR WORK.** **With a partner, find the answers to these questions in the conversation.**

1. What mistake does Paul think Matt is making?

2. Why won't Matt ask his parents for permission?

3. Do you agree or disagree with Paul? Explain your answer.

WHAT ABOUT **YOU?**

In your opinion, what should teenagers have to get permission for? Write yes, no, or it depends. Explain.

1. getting a tattoo:

_____

2. using makeup:

_____

3. changing hairstyles:

_____

4. face or body piercing:

_____

5. coming home late:

_____

DISCUSSION. **Do teenagers and their parents usually have the same ideas about getting permission? Support your opinion with examples from real life.**

Return Someone Else's Property

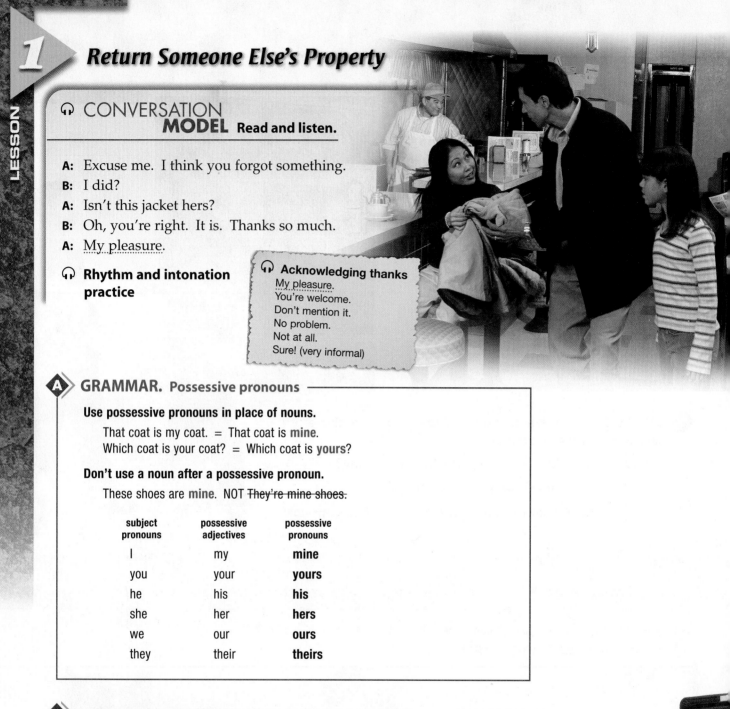

⌒ CONVERSATION
MODEL Read and listen.

A: Excuse me. I think you forgot something.
B: I did?
A: Isn't this jacket hers?
B: Oh, you're right. It is. Thanks so much.
A: My pleasure.

⌒ **Rhythm and intonation practice**

⌒ **Acknowledging thanks**
My pleasure.
You're welcome.
Don't mention it.
No problem.
Not at all.
Sure! (very informal)

A GRAMMAR. Possessive pronouns

Use possessive pronouns in place of nouns.

That coat is my coat. = That coat is **mine**.
Which coat is your coat? = Which coat is **yours**?

Don't use a noun after a possessive pronoun.

These shoes are **mine**. NOT ~~They're mine shoes.~~

subject pronouns	possessive adjectives	possessive pronouns
I	my	**mine**
you	your	**yours**
he	his	**his**
she	her	**hers**
we	our	**ours**
they	their	**theirs**

B Rewrite the following sentences. Substitute possessive pronouns for the highlighted phrases.

1. Those gloves are my gloves. *Those gloves are mine* _____.

2. That is her coat. _____.

3. The books on that table are Daniel's books. _____.

4. Their car and our car are parked on the same street. _____.

5. Are those my tickets or her tickets? _____?

6. The white house is my mother's house. _____.

7. Is this painting your painting or her brother's painting?

   _____?

C **Complete the following statements and questions. Choose the right answer.**

1. **A:** Whose umbrella is this, _____ or _____?
   <u>he / his</u>   <u>her / hers</u>

   B: I'm not sure. Ask them if it's _____.
   <u>their / theirs</u>

2. **A:** Who is stricter? Your parents or Jerome's?

   B: _____, I think. _____ parents aren't strict at all.
   <u>He / His</u>   <u>My / Mine</u>

3. **A:** Is this _____ suitcase?
   <u>ours / our</u>

   B: No, I already have _____ suitcase, so this one can't be _____.
   <u>our / ours</u>   <u>our / ours</u>

4. **A:** I found this bracelet on the bus. Is it _____?
   <u>her / hers</u>

   B: No, it's _____ bracelet. I'm so happy someone found it!
   <u>my / mine</u>

5. **A:** Is that _____ car?
   <u>their / theirs</u>

   B: No, _____ is the black one over there.
   <u>their / theirs</u>

6. **A:** Where should we meet? At _____ house or _____?
   <u>your / yours</u>   <u>my / mine</u>

   B: Neither. Let's meet at _____ office.
   <u>my / mine</u>

CONVERSATION
PAIR WORK

Collect personal items to use in the pair work, or use the pictures. In pairs or groups of three, return something that belongs to someone else. Start like this:

A: Excuse me. I think you forgot something.

B: I did?

A: _____?

B: _____.

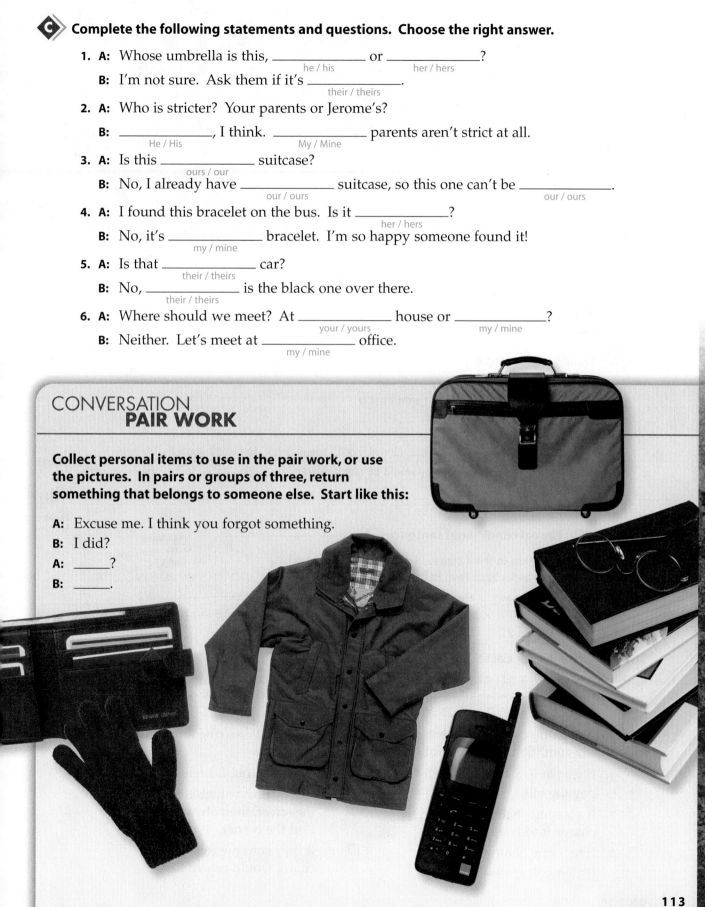

2 · Discuss Ethical Choices

∩ CONVERSATION MODEL Read and listen.

A: Look at this. They didn't charge us for the desserts.
B: Really? We'd better tell the waiter.
A: You think so?
B: Absolutely. If we didn't tell him, it would be wrong.

∩ **Rhythm and intonation practice**

∩ **Confirming responses**
Absolutely.
Definitely.
Of course.
Sure.

A GRAMMAR. Factual and unreal conditional sentences: meaning

Factual conditionals: present
If I **eat** too much, I **gain** weight.
If you **speak** English, you **can speak** to people all over the world.

Factual conditionals: future
If I **ask** my parents for permission, they**'ll say** no.
If they **tell** me getting a tattoo is wrong, I **won't get** one.

Unreal conditionals: present
If I **spoke** Greek, I **would apply** for that job. (unreal: I don't speak Greek, so I won't apply for the job.)
If her parents **knew** about her tattoo, they **would be** angry. (unreal: They don't know, so they are not angry.)

PAGES G19–20
For more...

B GRAMMAR. Unreal conditional sentences: form

Use the simple past tense in the if clause. For the verb be, always use were. Use would and a base form in the result clause.

if clause (unreal condition)	result clause (unreal result)
If Paul **pierced** his ears,	his father **would be** angry.
If Marie **were** 21,	she **would pierce** her ears.

Don't use would in the if clause.
If I **found** a wallet, I would return it. NOT If I ~~would find~~ a wallet, I would return it.

Questions
Would you ask your parents if you wanted a tattoo?
What would you do if you were 21?

PAGE G21
For more ...

C Read the following conditional sentences. Check the ones that describe an unreal condition (a condition that does not exist).

☐ **1.** If we eat in a restaurant, I'll pay the bill.
☐ **2.** If you get a haircut, you can charge it to your room.
☐ **3.** If he came home really late, his parents would worry.
☐ **4.** If I were you, I'd tell the truth.
☐ **5.** If they find valuable things on the street, they always try to find the owner.
☐ **6.** If they sent me the wrong coat, I would return it.

D Complete each unreal conditional sentence with the correct form of the verb.

1. If I _____ tickets, I _____ to the concert at the mall.
   (have)   (go)

2. If his father _____ angry, he _____ off the earrings.
   (get)   (take)

3. If the check _____ not correct, she _____ it.
   (be)   (not pay)

4. If they _____ the wrong package, they _____ the mail-order company.
   (receive)   (call)

5. If I _____ the best place to get my ears pierced, I _____ there.
   (know)   (go)

E 🎧 **PRONUNCIATION.** Assimilation of sounds. **Notice how /d/ + /y/ becomes /dʒ/. Listen and repeat.**

1. What would you do if you found a wallet on the street?
2. What would you do if the waiter didn't charge you for the dessert?
3. Who would you call if you were sick?
4. Where would you go if you wanted a great meal?

F 🎧 **VOCABULARY.** Some moral dilemmas. **Listen and practice.**

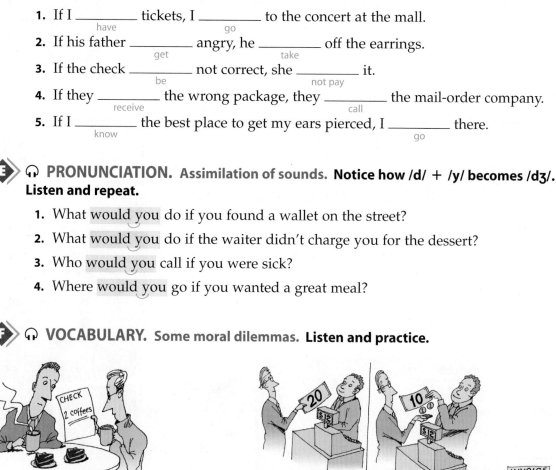

They didn't charge us for the cake.

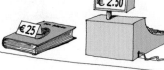

They undercharged me.

They gave me too much change.

They gave me more than I ordered.

CONVERSATION
PAIR WORK

Discuss ethical choices. Use the guide and the situations, or use your <u>own</u> ideas.

A: Look. _____.
B: _____? We'd better _____.
A: You think so?
B: _____. If we _____, _____.

You see money on the floor near a man who is putting his wallet into his pocket. You are pretty sure the money fell out of his wallet.

You see an expensive suit with a mistake on the price tag. The suit should cost twice as much.

You look at the check for a restaurant meal. They didn't charge you enough.

CONTROLLED PRACTICE

3 Express Personal Values

LESSON

A 🎧 **LISTENING COMPREHENSION.** **Listen to the conversations.**
Check <u>true</u> (T) or <u>false</u> (F).

         T F

1. ☐ ☐ **a.** Beth thinks it's OK for Luke to wear an earring to the office.
      ☐ ☐ **b.** Luke agrees with Beth.

2. ☐ ☐ **a.** Celia's husband has a tattoo.
      ☐ ☐ **b.** Celia's husband likes Celia's tattoo.

3. ☐ ☐ **a.** His daughter married a lawyer.
      ☐ ☐ **b.** He wants his daughter to stay home and have children.

4. ☐ ☐ **a.** Kate's dad likes the way Kate is dressed.
      ☐ ☐ **b.** Kate's dad thinks girls don't have to be modest.

B **Read the following quotations from the conversations.
Then choose the correct definition for the underlined
word or phrase. Listen again if necessary.**

1. "But lots of people are <u>old-fashioned</u>, and they
   don't think men should wear earrings."
   a. have ideas from the past
   b. don't like traditions

2. "What <u>a double standard</u>!"
   a. the same rules for all people
   b. different rules for different people

3. "That's a little <u>sexist</u>, if you ask me!"
   a. the idea that men and women are not equal
   b. the idea that men and women are equal

4. "But <u>modesty</u> is very important for girls."
   a. wearing clothes that cover their bodies
   b. wearing clothes that show their bodies

C **PAIR WORK.** **Think of an example for each word or phrase.
Write your ideas in the chart. Share your ideas with a partner.**

> 66 A lot of people think it's
> OK for men to wear shorts,
> but not for women. 99

old-fashioned	
a double standard	
sexist	
modesty	

STEP 1. Fill out the Values Self-Test. Then discuss with your partner.

VALUES SELF-TEST

Check the boxes that best describe <u>your</u> values. Include a specific example.

❏ I'm modern in my attitudes about modesty.
❏ I'm old-fashioned in my attitudes about modesty.

Explain _____

_____

❏ I think tattoos and body piercing are OK for men.
❏ I think tattoos and body piercing are OK for women.

Explain _____

_____

❏ I think it's OK to have a double standard for different people.
❏ I think the rules should be the same for everyone.

Explain _____

_____

❏ Some people might say I'm sexist.
❏ Nobody would say I'm sexist.

Explain _____

_____

STEP 2. DISCUSSION. Discuss one or more of the following questions.
Give reasons and examples.

1. Is it sometimes OK to have a double standard
for men and women?

2. Can people be sexist when they talk about
men, or only about women?

3. Are old-fashioned ideas usually better or
worse than modern ideas?

STEP 3. WRITING. On a separate sheet of
paper, write your ideas about modesty
and personal appearance. How should
men dress? How should women dress?

Man measuring the length of woman's
swimsuit in the 1920s (U.S.)

FREE PRACTICE

A **READING WARM-UP.** Do you know what a lost-and-found is?
Is there one in your city or town? Where?

B 🎧 **READING.** Read the article about the Tokyo lost-and-found.

Tokyo Lost-and-Found
KEEPS EYE ON GOODS

TOKYO—If it can be lost on the streets of Tokyo, it can be found in the city's cavernous lost-and-found center, where everything from diamond rings to dentures and millions of dollars in stray cash await their rightful, if forgetful, owners. On any given day, about 800,000 items pack the four-story warehouse, with 5,000 new ones trucked in every

Everything from diamond rings to dentures...

morning for an annual haul of 220,000 articles of clothing, 30,000 mobile phones, 18,000 eyeglasses, and 17,000 wallets.

"I'm not surprised anymore by what people lose," says custodian Nobuo Hasuda as he walks along the paths between wheelchairs, snowshoes, motorcycle

...30,000 mobile phones, 18,000 eyeglasses, and 17,000 wallets...

helmets, and trumpets. There are file cabinets labeled "Mobile Phones: April," "Wallets: March," and "Eyeglasses: February."

Last year, about 1.62 million articles passed through the center, making it possibly the world's biggest lost-and-found. About 250 hopefuls visit each day to see if their lost keys, briefcases, and billfolds are there.

Typical of a country obsessed with order and detail, every item is scrupulously labeled with time and place of recovery, then computer archived—no matter how seemingly trivial. One Good Samaritan turned in a phone card worth only 42 cents. It's now tagged and waiting in a drawer cluttered with half-used train passes.

...wheelchairs, snowshoes, motorcycle helmets, and trumpets...

SOURCE: The Daily Mail www.dailymailnews.com

C **Answer the following questions.**

1. Have you ever found something you lost at a lost-and-found?
2. Would you take something you found to a lost-and-found?

D **PAIR WORK.** Which of these articles would <u>you</u> take to a lost-and-found? Which ones would you <u>not</u> take there? Explain your answers.

a diamond ring	a set of dentures	a cell phone
a pair of eyeglasses	a wallet	a wheelchair
a snowshoe	a trumpet	a motorcycle helmet

E **DISCUSSION.** What do most people do when they find something valuable? Do you think most people are honest?

TOP NOTCH
INTERACTION • *What would YOU do?*

STEP 1. Look at the situations. Answer the questions on the notepads.

Situation: You find a wallet full of cash.
What could you do?
What should you do?
What would you do?
What would most people do?

Situation: You find a gold watch in a department store dressing room.
What could you do?
What should you do?
What would you do?
What would most people do?

Situation: The cashier undercharges you.
What could you do?
What should you do?
What would you do?
What would most people do?

Situation: You find cash near an ATM.
What could you do?
What should you do?
What would you do?
What would most people do?

STEP 2. DISCUSSION. Discuss what you wrote about each situation.
Would you do what most people would do?

❝If I found the wallet, I would call the person on the phone. It would be wrong to keep the money.❞

❝If I found cash near an ATM, I would keep it. There would be no way to find the owner.❞

FREE PRACTICE

119

A 🎧 **LISTENING COMPREHENSION. Listen to the conversations and check the statements that are true.**

1. ☐ John doesn't think his grandmother is too old for a tattoo.
   ☐ John has a double standard.

2. ☐ Jessica and her mother are discussing Jessica's rules.
   ☐ Jessica thinks her mother is sexist.

3. ☐ Emily and Robert are discussing right and wrong.
   ☐ The waiter charged Emily and Robert too much for their dinner.

> **TOP NOTCH PROJECT**
> To help visitors understand appropriate appearance in your country, find pictures in magazines or newspapers that depict appropriate and inappropriate appearance. Make a do's and don'ts book.

> **TOP NOTCH WEBSITE**
> For Unit 10 online activities, visit the *Top Notch* Companion Website at www.longman.com/topnotch.

B **Rewrite sentences with possessive pronouns.**

1. Those shoes belong to my daughter.   *They're hers*_____.

2. That coat belongs to my son.   _____.

3. The house across the street is my parents' house.   _____.

4. These coins are my husband's and mine.   _____.

5. The table over there is your table.   _____.

C **Complete each conditional sentence. Use your <u>own</u> words.**

1. If the weather is bad this weekend, _____.

2. If _____, I'll go out to eat tonight.

3. If I found your wallet, _____.

4. If _____, I always call home.

5. If I had a new car, _____.

D **What would <u>you</u> do? Write an unreal conditional sentence beginning with <u>If</u>.**

1. You have two sandwiches for lunch, but they only charge you for one.
   If _____.

2. You pay for a newspaper that costs one dollar with a five-dollar bill.
   The merchant gives you nine dollars change.
   If _____.

3. You order a PDA from a mail-order company. You see that
   there are two PDAs and a cell phone in the box.
   If _____.

E **WRITING. On a separate sheet of paper, write a story about a time you or someone else had to make an ethical choice.**

UNIT WRAP-UP

- **Narration.** Tell a story, using the pictures.
- **Grammar.** Write what you would do in this situation.
- **Social language.** Create conversations for the people.

✔ *Now I can ...*

☐ return someone else's property.
☐ discuss ethical choices.
☐ express personal values.
☐ discuss honesty.

121

This is an alphabetical list of all productive vocabulary in the *Top Notch 2* units. The numbers refer to the page on which the word first appears or is defined. When a word has two meanings, both are in the list. Entries for 2A are in black. Entries for 2B are in blue.

A

a lot of   53
accident   40
addict   66
address people   2
afraid of   78
agree   23
air-conditioned   39
airport shuttle   27
aisle   52
allergic to   64
almost   100
already   7
always   16
angry about   78
animated film   18
any   53
anyone   54
apologize for   78
appointment   54
art exhibition   5
as   100
asparagus   65
automatic transmission   39
avoid   64

B

babysitting   27
before   7
believe in   78
bell service   27
birth order   82
blue   75
body lotion   52
bored with   78
boring   20
bow   2
bowl   90
brake   40
brand   51
bring up (a newspaper)   32
brush   52
bumper   40
business card   2
business center   31

C

calm   77
can't stand   66

CD drive   98
cell phone   118
charge   115
charming   82
cheer (someone) up   75
cheerful   77
chewy   70
chocolate   65
clay   90
click on (an icon)   102
climb   6
cloth   90
clown   82
clutch   40
comb   52
comedy   18
compact car   44
complain about   78
convertible   44
cool   90
copy text   102
cosmetic surgery   58
crash   102
crazy about   66
create a web page   104
creative   82
crunchy   70
cut off other drivers   47
cut text   102

D

damage   40
dashboard   40
definitely   66
dental floss   52
dentures (a set of)   118
deodorant   52
depressing   77
diamond ring   118
disagree   23
disgusting   77
documentary   18
don't agree with me   64
don't care for   64
door (car)   40
double room   30
double standard   116
down   75
down in the dumps   75

download   99
drama   18
drawing   87
driver's license   39
drop off   42

E

emergency brake   40
emotions   80
engine   40
environment   80
ever   7
exchange   2
excited about   78
exciting   77
extra   32
extrovert   81
eyeglasses (a pair of)   118

F

facial   56
familiar   4
fantastic   90
fascinated by   94
fashion   87
feel 23
figure   90
fill up   42
film   87
fitness center   31
flash lights   47
for   16
fries   65
full-size car   44
funny   20

G

game   98
gas pedal   40
gearshift   40
genetics   80
gesture   8
get stuck in traffic   17
gift shop   31
glass   90
go sightseeing   6
go to the top of   6
gold   90
gorgeous   90

greetings   2
gym   5

H

had better   31
hair care   50
hair spray   52
hair dryer   32
haircut   54
hanger   32
happy   77
happy about   78
hard   70
headlight   40
headset   98
hers   112
his   112
honk   47
hood   40
horn   40
horror film   18
hug   2

I

ice cream   65
icon   102
influenced by   94
inspired by   94
instant message   99
interested in   94
Internet connection   27
introvert   81
iron   32

J

join a chat room   104
joystick   98
just   16

K

keyboard   98
king-size bed   30
kiss   2

L

last name   2
late   16
lately   16
laundry   27
lifestyle   65
look (like)   70

lose weight 64
lost-and-found 118
luxury car 44

M
ma'am 40
make up the room 32
makeup 52
mango 65
manicure 54
manual transmission 39
many 53
massage 56
medicine 50
message 28
microphone 98
mine 112
minibar 27
miss (the bus) 17
modesty 116
monitor 98
motorcycle helmet 118
mouse 98
moved by 94
much 53
museum 89
musical 18

N
nail care 53
nail clipper 52
nail file 52
nature 80
nearly 100
nervous 77
noodle 65
not pay attention 41
not signal 47
not stop 47
nurture 80

O
object to 78
old-fashioned 116
on a diet 64
only 16
open a file 102
opinion 111
ours 112
out of sorts 75
owe 16

P
painting 87
parking space 17
pasta 65
paste text 102

pedicure 54
permission 111
personality 80
photocopying 27
photography 87
pick up 42
pick up the laundry 32
pool 31
pottery 87
print a file 102
pull-down menu 102

Q
queen-size bed 30
quite 100

R
razor 52
razor blade 52
rearview mirror 40
rebel 82
recently 16
reservation 39
road sign 46
rollaway bed 30
romantic 20
room service 27

S
sad 77
sad about 78
salty 70
sardine 65
sauna 31
save a file 102
scan pictures 104
science fiction film (sci-fi) 18
scissors (a pair of) 52
scroll bar 102
scroll down 102
scroll up 102
sculpture 87
seat belt 40
sedan 44
select text 102
self-critical 82
send an attachment 104
send e-mails 105
sexist 116
shake hands 2
shampoo (product) 52
shampoo (service) 54
shave 54
shaving 50
shaving cream 52
shellfish 65

shoe shine 27
shower cap 52
sibling 82
sick of 78
side-view mirror 40
signal 40
silly 20
silver 90
since 16
single room 30
sir 40
skin care 50
skirt hanger 32
small talk 2
smell (like) 70
smoking/non-smoking 30
snowshoe 118
so far 16
soap 52
soft 70
software 98
some 53
someone 54
sour 70
speaker 98
speed 41
spicy 70
sports car 44
station wagon 44
steak 65
steering wheel 40
still 16
stone 90
suite 30
sunscreen 52
surf the Internet 104
sushi 65
SUV 44
sweet 70

T
tailgate 41
taillight 40
take a tour of 6
take away the dishes 32
take pictures of 6
talk about 78
talk on a cell phone 41
taste (like) 70
tattoo 111
terrific 66
theater 5
theirs 112
thermometer 52
think 23
thoughts 80

tip 56
tire 40
tired of 78
tofu 65
tool bar 102
tooth care 50
toothbrush 52
toothpaste 52
towel 32
traffic 17
treat 16
trumpet 118
trunk 40
try 6
turn down the beds 32
turn off 42
turn on 42
twin bed 30

U
undercharge 115
unforgettable 20
used to 67

V
values 82
van 44
vase 90
vegetarian 64
violence 22
violent 20

W
wake-up service 27
wallet 118
weave through traffic 47
weird 20
wheelchair 118
why don't 65
will 28
window (car) 40
windshield 40
windshield wiper 40
wonderful 90
wood 90
worry about 78
would rather 19
wrong 111

Y
yet 7
yours 112

Social language list for 2A and 2B

This is a unit-by-unit list of all the productive social language from *Top Notch 2*.

Unit 1

You look familiar.
Have we met before?
I don't think so.
I'm not from around here.
As a matter of fact, I am.
Oh, that's right! Now I remember.

What have you been up to?
Not much.
[Audrey], have you met [Hanah]?
[Hanah], I'd like you to meet [Audrey].
I think we've met before.
Good to see you again.

Welcome to [Rio].
Have you ever been here before?
No. It's my first time.
Have you tried [feijoada] yet?
I think you'll like it.

Unit 2

You're going to love [this theater].
I'm really in the mood for [a good classic movie].
I missed it.
They say it's [great].
Actually, I'd rather see something else.
Deal!
Sorry I'm late. Have you been here long?
For about [10] minutes. Not too bad.
I got stuck in traffic.
I missed the bus.

I couldn't get a taxi.
I couldn't find a parking space.
The [8:00] show for [*The Train*] is sold out.
How much do I owe?
Nothing. It's on me.
Next time it's my treat.
I've always wanted to see [Hitchcock's *The Birds*].
What would you rather see—a [comedy] or a [musical]?
It doesn't matter to me.

What do you think of [Madonna]?
Actually, not much.
For real? (to express surprise)
That's what makes the world go 'round!
Who was in it?
What was it about?
What kind of movie was it?
Was it good?
Do you recommend it?
I agree / disagree.

Unit 3

I'm checking out.
Was your stay satisfactory?
Will you be putting this on your [Vista card]?
Thank you for staying with us.
I'd like to speak to [Anne Smith].
I'll ring that room for you.

He's / She's not answering.
Would you like to leave a message?
Please tell him [Tim Klein] called.
Please tell her I'll call back later.
Please tell him I'll be [at the Clayton Hotel] until [5:00].
Please tell her I'll be at [22-56-838]
Is that all?

I'm checking in. The name's [Smith].
How do you want to pay?
By the way, is the [restaurant] still open?
Actually, you'd better hurry.

Unit 4

I have a reservation.
We were expecting you.
I'll need to see your [driver's license and a major credit card].
That's correct.
That'll be fine.
I had an accident.
How awful.
Oh no!
I'm sorry to hear that.
I'm so sorry. Are you OK?
No one was hurt.

Thank goodness. How did it happen?
[The other driver] was [speeding].
I hit another car. / Another car hit me.
Was there much damage?
I'll only have to replace [a taillight].
Fill it up, please, with [regular].
Yes, sir / ma'am.
Anything else?
My [turn signal] isn't working. Can you fix it?
Can you drop the car off [tomorrow morning] at about [9:00]?

What time can I pick it up?
How's [noon]?
Terrific. I'll see you at [9:00].
[My headlight] won't turn on / turn off.
[My car trunk] won't open / close.
[My engine] is making a funny sound.
[My headlight] isn't working.
[My car window] is stuck.

Unit 5

I need to pick up a few things on the way back to [the hotel].
Feel like stopping at [a cosmetics store] with me?
I'd like to, but I think I'll pass.
I don't have much time today.
It'll be a piece of cake.
Where would I find [toothpaste]?
Have a look in [aisle 2].

Actually, I did and there wasn't any.
Let me get you some from the back.
I have [a two o'clock] appointment for a [haircut] with [Sean].
[Sean] is running a little late.
Can I get you some [coffee] or [tea]?
Can I get a [manicure] in the meantime?
Yes, but it'll be a few minutes.
There's someone ahead of you.

Would it be possible to get a [facial]?
I don't have an appointment.
How long will I have to wait?
How much do you charge for a [massage]?
Is it customary to leave a tip?
Can I charge it to my room?
I'm sorry. I have to cancel my appointment.

Unit 6

What in the world are you [eating]?
I used to be. Not anymore.
To tell you the truth, it was just too much trouble.
Want to try some?
You only live once.
Everything's ready. Why don't we [sit down]?
This [food] looks great!
It really smells delicious.
Please help yourself.

Thanks. But I'll pass on the [chicken].
Don't you eat [chicken]?
I'm on a diet.
I'm trying to lose weight.
I'm avoiding [sugar].
I'm a vegetarian.
I'm allergic to [chocolate].
[Coffee] doesn't agree with me.
I'm sorry. I didn't know that.
Don't worry about it. It's not a problem.

I used to have it a lot. But I've been cutting back.
I couldn't live without it.
I'm [not] crazy about [seafood].
I'm a big [meat] eater / [coffee] drinker.
I'm a [chocolate] addict / [pizza] lover.
I can't stand [fish].
I don't care for [steak].
I'm not much of a [pizza] eater / [coffee] lover.

Unit 7

What do you feel like doing after dinner?
I'm kind of down in the dumps.
You (do) look a little blue. Something wrong?
Nothing I can put my finger on.
I guess I'm just feeling a little out of sorts.

Maybe [a nice dinner] will cheer you up.
Why don't we [go for a walk]?
Would you like me to [make you some soup]?
How about some [ice cream]? That always makes me feel better.
How about [gray]? (to talk about color preference)

[Gray]'s out of the question.
What's wrong with [gray]?
You look down. What's up?
Oh, nothing serious.
I'm just tired of the same old grind.
But thanks for asking.
I know what you mean.

Unit 8

This [print]'s sort of interesting.
I kind of like it.
It would look nice [over my desk].
Don't you find it a little too [dark]?
I guess I'm not really into [bright colors].
To each his own.
Be sure not to miss [the Prado Museum] while you're in [Madrid].
Really? Why's that?

Well, for one thing, [Las Meninas] is [kept] there.
No kidding! I've always wanted to see that.
Thanks for the suggestion.
What's this [figure] made of?
Wood. It's handmade.
What is it used for?
When were they made?

How were they made?
What do you think of it?
I'm not crazy about it / them.
I don't care for it / them.
It's not for me.
They're fantastic / gorgeous / wonderful / cool.

Unit 9

Am I interrupting you?
[I'm] just fooling around.
What are you up to?
I logged on to [send you some pictures].
Cool!
[I] can't wait to [download them].

I'm thinking about getting [a new monitor].
Oh, yeah? What kind?
Everyone says I should get [a Macro].
Well, I've heard that the [Panatel] is as [good] as the [Macro].

Really? I'll check it out.
[Eugene], could you take a look at this?
Sure. What's the problem?
Why don't you try [restarting]?
OK. I'll give that a try.

Unit 10

Your parents would let you do that?
Are you kidding?
I'd have to be nuts to [ask them].
There's nothing wrong with [tattoos]. Everybody has [them].
I hate to say this, but I think you're making a mistake.
You should get permission. If you don't, I'm sure you'll be sorry.

I'll give it some thought.
Excuse me, I think you forgot something.
My pleasure.
You're welcome.
Don't mention it.
Not at all.
Sure. (to acknowledge thanks)
They didn't charge us for the [desserts].

They undercharged me.
They gave me too much change.
They gave me more than I ordered.
You think so?
Absolutely.
Definitely.
Of course.
Sure. (to express certainty)

Pronunciation table

These are the pronunciation symbols used in *Top Notch 2*.

Vowels				Consonants			
Symbol	Key Word	Symbol	Key Word	Symbol	Key Word	Symbol	Key Word
i	beat, feed	ə	banana, among	p	pack, happy	z	zip, please, goes
ɪ	bit, did	ɚ	shirt, murder	b	back, rubber	ʃ	ship, machine, station, special, discussion
eɪ	date, paid	aɪ	bite, cry, buy, eye	t	tie		
ɛ	bet, bed	aʊ	about, how	d	die		
æ	bat, bad	ɔɪ	voice, boy	k	came, key, quick	ʒ	measure, vision
ɑ	box, odd, father	ɪr	deer	g	game, guest	h	hot, who
ɔ	bought, dog	ɛr	bare	tʃ	church, nature, watch	m	men
oʊ	boat, road	ɑr	bar			n	sun, know, pneumonia
ʊ	book, good	ɔr	door	dʒ	judge, general, major		
u	boot, food, flu	ʊr	tour			ŋ	sung, ringing
ʌ	but, mud, mother			f	fan, photograph	w	wet, white
				v	van	l	light, long
				θ	thing, breath	r	right, wrong
				ð	then, breathe	y	yes
				s	sip, city, psychology	t̬	butter, bottle
						t˺	button

Irregular verbs

base form	simple past	past participle	base form	simple past	past participle
be	was / were	been	leave	left	left
become	became	become	let	let	let
begin	began	begun	lose	lost	lost
break	broke	broken	make	made	made
bring	brought	brought	mean	meant	meant
build	built	built	meet	met	met
buy	bought	bought	pay	paid	paid
catch	caught	caught	put	put	put
choose	chose	chosen	quit	quit	quit
come	came	come	read /rid/	read /rɛd/	read /rɛd/
cost	cost	cost	ride	rode	ridden
cut	cut	cut	ring	rang	rung
do	did	done	rise	rose	risen
draw	drew	drawn	run	ran	run
dream	dreamed / dreamt	dreamed / dreamt	say	said	said
drink	drank	drunk	see	saw	seen
drive	drove	driven	sell	sold	sold
eat	ate	eaten	send	sent	sent
fall	fell	fallen	shake	shook	shaken
feed	fed	fed	sing	sang	sung
feel	felt	felt	sit	sat	sat
fight	fought	fought	sleep	slept	slept
find	found	found	speak	spoke	spoken
fit	fit	fit	spend	spent	spent
fly	flew	flown	stand	stood	stood
forget	forgot	forgotten	steal	stole	stolen
get	got	gotten	swim	swam	swum
give	gave	given	take	took	taken
go	went	gone	teach	taught	taught
grow	grew	grown	tell	told	told
have	had	had	think	thought	thought
hear	heard	heard	throw	threw	thrown
hit	hit	hit	understand	understood	understood
hold	held	held	wake up	woke up	woken up
hurt	hurt	hurt	wear	wore	worn
keep	kept	kept	win	won	won
know	knew	known	write	wrote	written

Verb tense review: present, past, and future

 THE PRESENT OF BE

Statements

I	am	
You We They	are	late.
He She It	is	

 THE SIMPLE PRESENT TENSE

Statements

I You We They	speak English.
He She	speaks English.

Yes / no questions

Do	I you we they	know them?
Does	he she	eat meat?

Short answers

Yes,	I you we they	do.
	he she it	does.

No,	I you we they	don't.
	he she it	doesn't.

Information questions

What do	you we they	need?
When does	he she it	start?
Who	wants needs likes	this book?

 **THE PRESENT CONTINUOUS**

Statements

I	am	watching TV.
You We They	are	studying English.
He She It	is	arriving now.

Yes / no questions

Am	I	
Are	you we they	going too fast?
Is	he she it	

Short answers

Yes,	I	am.
	you	are.
	he she it	is.
	we they	are.

No,	I'm not.
	you aren't / you're not.
	he isn't / he's not.
	she isn't / she's not.
	it isn't / it's not.
	we aren't / we're not.
	they aren't / they're not.

Information questions

What	are	you we they	doing?
When	is	he she it	leaving?
Where	am	I	staying tonight?
Who	is		driving?

4 **THE PAST OF BE**

Statements

I He She It	was late.
We You They	were early.

Yes / no questions

Was	I he she it	on time?
Were	we you they	in the same class?

Short answers

Yes,	I he she it	was.
	we you they	were.

No,	I he she it	wasn't.
	we you they	weren't.

Information questions

Where	were	we? you? they?	
When	was	he she it	here?
Who	were	they?	
Who	was	he? she? it?	

5 THE SIMPLE PAST TENSE

Many verbs are irregular in the simple past tense.
See the list of irregular verbs on page A5.

Statements

I You He She It We They	stopped working.

I You He She It We They	didn't start again.

Yes / no questions

Did	I you he she it we they	make a good dinner?

Short answers

Yes,	I you he she it we they	did.

No,	I you he she it we they	didn't.

Information questions

When did	I you he she it we they	read that?
Who		called?

6 THE FUTURE WITH BE GOING TO

Statements

I'm You're He's She's It's We're They're	going to	be here soon.

I'm You're He's She's It's We're They're	not going to	be here soon.

Yes / no questions

Are	you we they	going to want coffee?
Am	I	going to be late?
Is	he she it	going to arrive on time?

Short answers

Yes,	I	am.
	you	are.
	he she it	is.
	we they	are.

No,	I'm not.
	you aren't / you're not.
	he isn't / he's not.
	she isn't / she's not.
	it isn't / it's not.
	we aren't / we're not.
	they aren't / they're not.

Information questions

What	are	you we they	going to see?
When	is	he she it	going to shop?
Where	am	I	going to stay tomorrow?
Who	is		going to call?

GRAMMAR
BOOSTER

2B

GRAMMAR BOOSTER

The *Grammar Booster* is optional. It provides more explanation and practice, as well as additional grammar concepts.

UNIT 6   Lesson 1

Negative yes / no questions: short answers

Answer negative yes / no questions the same way as you would answer other yes / no questions.

Is Jane a vegetarian?
Isn't Jane a vegetarian?
} Yes, she is. / No, she isn't.

Do they have two sons?
Don't they have two sons?
} Yes, they do. / No, they don't.

A ⟩ **Read the information. Answer the negative question with a short answer.**

1. (Hank is not a lawyer.)

   A: Isn't Hank a lawyer? **B:** _____.

2. (Bob has two younger brothers and an older sister.)

   A: Doesn't Bob have two younger brothers and an older sister? **B:** _____.

3. (You have never been to Siberia.)

   A: Haven't you been to Siberia before? **B:** _____.

4. (You're learning English right now.)

   A: Aren't you learning English right now? **B:** _____.

5. (Nancy didn't go to the movie theater last night.)

   A: Wasn't Nancy at the movie theater last night? **B:** _____.

Why don't …? / Why doesn't …?

Make suggestions with Why don't …? or Why doesn't …?

A: It's cold.	**B:** Why don't you put on a sweater?
A: The play's at 8:00.	**B:** Why don't we leave early?
A: My daughter has a toothache.	**B:** Why doesn't she see a dentist?

B ⟩ **Write a suggestion with Why don't …? or Why doesn't …? for each situation.**

1. "I'm not feeling well."

   ⟨YOU⟩ _____.

2. "I'm in the mood for seafood."

   ⟨YOU⟩ _____.

3. "My teacher works very hard. He hasn't taken a vacation for a long time."

   ⟨YOU⟩ _____.

4. "My neighbor can't open her door. The key is stuck."

   ⟨YOU⟩ _____.

5. "It's such a beautiful day. I don't want to stay indoors."

   ⟨YOU⟩ _____.

UNIT 6   Lesson 2

Used to: form

In questions and negative statements, <u>used to</u> becomes <u>use to</u>.

When you were a kid, **did** you **use to** like vegetables?
When I was a kid, I **didn't use to** like vegetables. I only used to like candy.

A **Write a <u>yes</u> / <u>no</u> question for each statement.**

1. I used to go running every day.

   Did you use to go running every day?

2. There used to be a large tree in front of my house.

   _____

3. Mr. and Mrs. Palmer used to go dancing every weekend.

   _____

4. My grandmother used to put sugar in our orange juice.

   _____

5. Luke used to be very heavy.

   _____

B **On a separate sheet of paper, write each sentence with a negative or affirmative form of <u>used to</u>.**

1. Jason and Trish / get lots of exercise, but now they go swimming every day.

2. There / be a movie theater on Smith Street, but now there isn't.

3. Nobody / worry about fatty foods, but now most people do.

4. English / be an international language, but now everyone uses English to communicate around the world.

5. Women / wear pants, but now it's very common.

UNIT 7   Lesson 1

Gerunds and infinitives

A gerund (an **–ing** form of a verb) functions as a noun. Gerunds can be subjects, objects, or subject complements.

> **Painting** is my favorite leisure-time activity. (subject)
> I love **painting**. (direct object)
> I read a book about the history of **painting**. (object of the preposition <u>of</u>)
> My favorite activity is **painting**. (subject complement)

An infinitive (<u>to</u> + the base form of a verb) also functions as a noun.

> **To paint** well is a talent. (subject)
> I love **to paint**. (direct object)
> The only thing he likes is **to paint**. (subject complement)

A ▶ **Underline the gerunds and circle the infinitives in the following sentences.**

1. I love watching DVDs, and I like to sing too.

2. Avoiding sweets makes a healthy change in your diet.

3. The most important thing I do is cooking dinner for my children.

4. What's the point of inviting her to the movies?

5. They're always angry about our leaving the lights on late.

6. Last year I devoted myself to studying English.

Gerunds and infinitives after certain verbs

Certain verbs are followed by gerunds:
avoid, can't help, can't stand, consider, discuss, dislike, enjoy, feel like, finish, (don't) mind, practice, quit, suggest.

Certain verbs are followed by infinitives:
agree, be sure, choose, decide, expect, hope, learn, need, plan, promise, refuse, seem, want, wish, would like.

Other verbs can be followed by either a gerund or an infinitive:
begin, continue, hate, like, love, prefer, start.

B ▸ **Complete each sentence with a gerund or an infinitive.**

Let me tell you something about my husband. He enjoys _____ early and
                                                                    1. get up
_____ in the park. He doesn't mind _____, even when the weather is
     2. run   3. go
bad. On the mornings when he doesn't feel like _____, he sleeps late. One day, I
                                                              4. exercise
would like _____ him when he exercises.
                 5. join
    I actually prefer _____ to bed late, and I love _____ until
                            6. go   7. read
midnight. But now I plan _____ that habit. From tomorrow on, I want
                                      8. stop
_____ to sleep early, even though I hate _____ that. We talked about it,
      9. go   10. do
and I agreed _____ my daily routine and _____ running with him for
                    11. change   12. go
one week.

UNIT 7   Lesson 2

┌─ **Negative gerunds** ──
│
│ **A gerund can be made negative by using a negative word before it.**
│   I like **not going** to bed too late.
│   They complained about **never having** enough time.
│
└──

A ▸ **Complete the following paragraph with affirmative and negative gerunds.**

I really want to do something to improve my appearance and lose weight. First of all,
I'm sick of _____ able to fit into my clothes. I want to go on a diet, but I'm afraid
                   1. be
of _____ hungry all the time. I can't complain about _____ in shape
      2. feel   3. stay
because right now I spend every afternoon _____ my bike. However, I do worry
                                                         4. ride
about _____ enough energy to exercise if I've had a few days of _____
           5. have   6. get
enough to eat.

UNIT 8 Lesson 1

The passive voice: form

Many sentences can be written in both active voice or passive voice. Form the passive voice with a form of <u>be</u> and the past participle of the verb.

	ACTIVE VOICE	PASSIVE VOICE
simple present tense	Art collectors **buy** famous paintings all over the world.	Famous paintings **are bought by** art collectors all over the world.
present continuous	The Film Center **is showing** Kurosawa's films.	Kurosawa's films **are being shown** at the Film Center.
present perfect	World leaders **have bought** Yu Hung's paintings.	Yu Hung's paintings **have been bought** by world leaders.
simple past tense	I.M. Pei **designed** the Grand Pyramid at the Louvre.	The Grand Pyramid at the Louvre **was designed** by I.M. Pei.
past continuous	Last year, the museum **was selling** copies of Monet's paintings.	Last year, copies of Monet's paintings **were being sold** by the museum.
future with <u>will</u>	Ang Lee **will direct** a new film next year.	A new film **will be directed** by Ang Lee next year.
future with <u>be going to</u>	The Tate Gallery **is going to show** Van Gogh's *Sunflowers* next month.	Van Gogh's *Sunflowers* **is going to be shown** at the Tate Gallery next month.

The passive voice: use

The active voice focuses on the "doer" of the action. Use the passive voice to focus on the "receiver" of the action.

A Japanese art collector   bought   Van Gogh's portrait of Dr. Gachet.

Van Gogh's portrait of Dr. Gachet   was bought by   a Japanese art collector.

Use the passive voice when:

a. the person or thing doing the action is not known or not important.

> Ceramic pottery **is made** in many parts of the world.

b. the person or thing doing the action is clear from context.

> Frida Kahlo did a lot of painting after her accident. A number of her self-portraits **were painted** at that time.

The <u>by</u> phrase
Use a <u>by</u> phrase in passive voice sentences when it is important to know who is performing an action.

The *Mona Lisa* was painted **by Leonardo Da Vinci**.   (important)
This stone carving was found (by someone) in Costa Rica.   (not important)

The passive voice: intransitive verbs

Intransitive verbs don't have objects. With intransitive verbs, there is no "receiver" of an action. For that reason, intransitive verbs are not used in the passive voice.

John **arrives** tomorrow. Janet **came** to the party. We **live** in an apartment.

Some common intransitive verbs:

die	happen	rain	sleep	arrive	fall	laugh	
seem	stand	come	go	live	sit	stay	walk

A On a separate sheet of paper, rewrite the sentences that have transitive verbs, changing them from the active voice into the passive voice.

1. Pedro Almodóvar is directing a new film about women.

2. A Canadian art collector has bought two of Michelangelo's drawings.

3. Someone stole Edvard Munch's painting *The Scream* in 2004.

4. The painter Georgia O'Keeffe lived in the southwestern part of the United States for many years.

5. The Van Gogh Museum in Amsterdam will send *Sunflowers* on tour.

6. The British Museum has bought some new sculptures for its ancient Roman collection.

7. The Metropolitan Museum of Art is going to open a new gallery next year.

B On a separate sheet of paper, rewrite these sentences in the passive voice. Use a <u>by</u> phrase only if it is important to know who is performing the action.

1. Someone actually stole the *Mona Lisa* in 1911.

2. Paloma Picasso designed these pieces of jewelry.

3. People built great pyramids throughout Central America during the height of the Mayan civilization.

4. Someone will repair the sculpture when it gets old.

5. People have paid millions of U.S. dollars for Van Gogh's paintings.

6. Hmong people from Laos made this colorful cloth.

UNIT 8 Lesson 2

The passive voice: questions

To form <u>yes</u> / <u>no</u> questions in the passive voice, move the first auxiliary verb before the subject.

simple present tense	**Are** famous paintings ~~are~~ **bought** by art collectors?
present continuous	**Are** Kurosawa's films ~~are~~ **being shown** at the Film Center?
present perfect	**Have** Yu Hung's paintings ~~have~~ **been bought** by world leaders?
simple past tense	**Was** the Grand Pyramid at the Louvre ~~was~~ **designed** by I.M. Pei?
past continuous	**Were** copies of Monet's paintings ~~were~~ **being sold** by the museum?
future with <u>will</u>	**Will** a new film ~~will~~ **be directed** by Ang Lee next year?
future with <u>be going to</u>	**Is** Van Gogh's *Sunflowers* ~~is~~ **going to be shown** at the Tate Gallery next month?

A **On a separate sheet of paper, rewrite the sentences as <u>yes</u> / <u>no</u> questions in the passive voice.**

1. That new film about families is being directed by Gillian Armstrong.

2. One of Da Vinci's most famous drawings has been sold by a German art collector.

3. A rare ceramic figure from the National Palace Museum in Taipei will be sent to the Metropolitan Museum of Art in New York.

4. A new exhibit is going to be opened at the Photography Gallery this week.

5. Some new paintings have been bought by the Prado Museum for their permanent collection.

6. *Las Meninas* can be seen at the Prado Museum in Madrid.

7. The *Jupiter* Symphony was written by Mozart.

8. Some of Michelangelo's work was being shown around the world in the 1960s.

UNIT 9 Lesson 1

Comparison with adjectives: review

Comparatives
Use comparatives to show how two things are different in degree.

My laptop is **lighter than** John's (is).

Superlatives
Use superlatives to show how one thing is different from two or more other things.

The M12, LX, and Pell monitors are all good monitors. But the Pell is **the best**.

<u>as</u> ... <u>as</u>
Use <u>as</u> ... <u>as</u> to show that two things are equal. Use the negative form to show that two things are different.

The new X12 monitor is **as big as** the old X10 model. (They're the same size.)

The Perk monitor is **not as big as** the X12. (They're of different sizes.)

A **Each sentence has one error. Correct the error.**

1. The Ortman headset isn't as clearer as the Pike headset.

2. My old laptop didn't have as many problems than my new laptop.

3. I checked out the three top brands, and the Piston was definitely the better.

4. Maxwell's web camera is much more expensive as their digital camera.

5. Of all the monitors I looked at, the X60 is definitely larger.

As ... as with adverbs

Adverbs often give information about verbs

My phone works **well**.   My printer prints **fast**.

Many adjectives can be changed to adverbs by adding –ly.

loud → loud**ly**   bad → bad**ly**

poor → poor**ly**   quiet → quiet**ly**

quick → quick**ly**   slow → slow**ly**

You can use as ... as with many adverbs.

My new phone works **as well as** my old one.
The Macro laptop doesn't run **as slowly as** the Pell laptop.

B **Read the statements. On a separate sheet of paper, write sentences with as ... as.**

1. My brother's MP3 player downloads quickly. My MP3 player also downloads quickly.

2. My new computer doesn't log on slowly. My old computer logs on slowly.

3. Your scanner works well. My scanner also works well.

4. The Rico printer prints quickly. The Grant printer doesn't print quickly.

5. The Pax CD drive doesn't run quietly. The Rico CD drive runs quietly.

UNIT 9 *Lesson 2*

Expressing purpose with in order to

You can use in order to to express purpose. The following three sentences have the same meaning:

I scrolled down **because I wanted to** read the text.
I scrolled down **in order to** read the text.
I scrolled down **to** read the text.

A On a separate sheet of paper, rewrite the sentences with <u>in order to</u>.

1. I joined a chat room to meet new people.

2. Jason surfs the Internet to find interesting websites.

3. Alison is instant messaging her friend Nancy to invite her for dinner.

4. They always print their files to read them.

5. I never use the pull-down menu to open a file.

> ┌─ Expressing purpose with <u>for</u> ──────────────────────
> **You can use <u>for</u> to express purpose. Use <u>for</u> before a noun.**
>
>   She e-mailed me **for some advice**.
>   They shop online **for electronics products**.
>
> **Never use <u>for</u> before an infinitive of purpose.**
>
>   DON'T SAY She e-mailed me ~~for~~ to ask a question.

B Complete each sentence with <u>for</u> or <u>to</u>.

1. My friend Jay e-mailed me _____ say he's getting married.

2. Matt created a web page _____ keep in touch with his family and friends.

3. I went online _____ find a new keyboard.

4. Jane shops online _____ clothing.

5. When Gina's computer crashed, her brother came to her apartment _____ help her.

6. Sometimes I use my computer _____ download music.

7. I designed a new home page _____ my company.

8. We both log on to the Internet _____ information.

UNIT 10 Lesson 2

> ┌─ Conditional sentences: meaning ──────────────────────
> **Conditional sentences express a result of an action. They usually have an <u>if</u> clause and a result clause.**
>
> | **<u>if</u> clause (the condition)** | **result clause** |
> |---|---|
> | If I eat dinner at home, | I don't eat too much. |
> | If they speak Dutch to the taxi driver, | he won't understand. |
> | If they had more money, | they would take a trip. |

A ▷ **Underline the result clause in each of the following sentences.**

1. If the weather is good, <u>I exercise outside</u>.
2. <u>I'm not happy</u> if I don't get enough sleep.
3. If they were extroverts, <u>they would talk more</u>.
4. <u>The students will start on Monday</u> if they get their books in time.

┌─ **Conditional sentences: present factual** ────────────────────

Use the present factual conditional to talk about general and scientific facts. Use the simple present tense or the present tense of <u>be</u> in both clauses.

    If it **rains**, flights **are** delayed. (general fact)
    If you **heat** water to 100 degrees, it **boils**. (scientific fact)

└──

B ▷ **Complete each present factual conditional sentence.**

1. Water _____ if you _____ its temperature below 0 degrees.
              freeze   lower

2. If I _____ something on the ground in the street, I _____ it to the owner.
       see   return

3. She _____ on vacation in August if she _____ too much work.
        go   not have

4. He _____ in the park if the weather _____ dry.
       run   be

┌─ **Conditional sentences: future factual** ────────────────────

Use the future factual conditional to talk about what will happen in the future under certain conditions. Use the simple present tense in the <u>if</u> clause. Use the future with <u>will</u> or <u>be going to</u> in the result clause.

    If I **go** to sleep too late tonight, I **won't be able to get up** on time. (future condition, future result)
    If she **comes** home after 8:00, I'm **not going to make** dinner. (future condition, future result)

Don't use a future form in the <u>if</u> clause.

    If I **see** him, I'll tell him. NOT If I ~~will~~ see him, I'll tell him.
                                   NOT If I'~~m going to~~ see him, I'll tell him.

└──

C ▷ **Choose the correct form to complete each future factual conditional sentence.**

1. If they _____ the movie, they _____ it again.
              like / will like   see / will see

2. I _____ to her if she _____ that again.
     'm going to talk / talk   does / 's going to do

3. If you _____ some eggs, I _____ you an omelet tonight.
       buy / are going to buy   make / 'll make

4. If they _____ her tomorrow, they _____ her home.
         see /will see   drive / 'll drive

5. _____ Italian if they _____ it next year?
     Are you going to study / Do you study   offer / will offer

┌─ **Conditional sentences: present unreal** ─────────────────────────────

Use the present unreal conditional to talk about unreal conditions and their results. Use the simple past tense in the <u>if</u> clause. For the verb <u>be</u>, always use <u>were</u>. Use <u>would</u> and a base form in the result clause.

> If I **had** black shoes, I **would wear** them. (But I don't have black shoes: unreal condition, unreal result.)
> If I **were** a teacher, I **would teach** French. (But I'm not a teacher: unreal condition, unreal result.)

Don't use <u>would</u> in the <u>if</u> clause.

> If I **knew** his name, I would tell you. NOT If I ~~would know~~ his name, I would tell you.
└──

 Complete each present unreal conditional sentence. Use your <u>own</u> ideas.

1. If I lived to be 100, _____.

2. My family would be angry if _____.

3. If I didn't study English, _____.

4. If I went to my favorite restaurant, _____.

5. If I were a child again, _____.

6. The English class would be better if _____.

┌─ **Conditional sentences: order of clauses** ───────────────────────────

In all conditional sentences, the clauses can be reversed with no change in meaning. In writing, use a comma between the clauses when the <u>if</u> clause comes first.

> If you don't return the bracelet, you'll feel bad.
> You'll feel bad if you don't return the bracelet.
└──

E **On a separate sheet of paper, rewrite all the sentences in exercises A–D, reversing the clauses and using commas where necessary.**

♫ TOP NOTCH POP LYRICS FOR 2A AND 2B

Greetings and Small Talk [Unit 1]

You look so familiar. Have we met before?
I don't think you're from around here.
It might have been two weeks ago, but I'm not sure.
Has it been a month or a year?
I have a funny feeling that I've met you twice.
That's what they call déjà vu.
You were saying something friendly, trying to be nice,
and now you're being friendly too.
One look, one word.
It's the friendliest sound that I've ever heard.
Thanks for your greeting.
I'm glad this meeting occurred.

(CHORUS)
Greetings and small talk
make the world go round.
On every winding road I've walked,
this is what I've found.

Have you written any letters to your friends back home?
Have you had a chance to do that?
Have you spoken to your family on the telephone?
Have you taken time for a chat?
Bow down, shake hands.
Do whatever you do in your native land.
I'll be happy to greet you
in any way that you understand.

(CHORUS)

Have you seen the latest movie out of Hollywood?
Have you read about it yet?
If you haven't eaten dinner, are you in the mood
for a meal you won't forget?
Bow down, shake hands.
Do whatever you do in your native land.
I'll be happy to greet you
in any way that you understand.

(CHORUS)

Better Late Than Never [Unit 2]

Where have you been? I've waited for you.
I'd rather not say how long.
The movie began one hour ago.
How did you get the time all wrong?
Well, I got stuck in traffic, and when I arrived,
I couldn't find a parking place.
Did you buy the tickets? You're kidding—for real?
Let me pay you back, in that case.

(CHORUS)
Sorry I'm late.
I know you've waited here forever.
How long has it been?
It's always better late than never.
When that kind of movie comes to the big screen,
it always attracts a crowd.
And I've always wanted to see it with you,
but it looks like we've missed it now.
I know what you're saying, but actually,
I would rather watch a video.
So why don't we rent it and bring it back home?
Let's get in the car and go.

(CHORUS)

Didn't you mention, when we made our plans,
that you've seen this movie recently?
It sounds so dramatic, and I'm so upset,
I'd rather see a comedy!
Well, which comedy do you recommend?
It really doesn't matter to me.
I still haven't seen *The World and a Day*.
I've heard that one is pretty funny.

(CHORUS)

Wheels around the World [Unit 4]

Was I going too fast
or a little too slow?
I was looking out the window,
and I just don't know.
I must have turned the steering wheel
a little too far
when I drove into the bumper
of that luxury car.
Oh no!
How awful!
What a terrible day!
I'm sorry to hear that.
Are you OK?

(CHORUS)
Wheels around the World
are waiting here with your car.
Pick it up.
Turn it on.
Play the radio.
Wheels around the World—
"helping you to go far."
You can drive anywhere.
Buckle up and go.

Did I hit the red sedan,
or did it hit me?
I was talking on the cell phone
in my SUV.
Nothing was broken,
and no one was hurt,
but I did spill some coffee
on my favorite shirt.
Oh no!
Thank goodness
you're still alive!
I'm so happy that
you survived.

(CHORUS)

What were you doing when you hit that tree?
I was racing down the mountain, and the brakes failed me.
How did it happen? Was the road still wet?
Well, there might have been a danger sign,
but I forget.
The hood popped open and the door fell off.
The headlights blinked and the engine coughed.
The side-view mirror had a terrible crack.
The gearshift broke. Can I bring the car back?
Oh no!
Thank goodness
you're still alive!
I'm so happy that
you survived.

(CHORUS)

The Colors of Love [Unit 7]

Are you sick and tired of working hard day and night?
Do you like to look at the world in shades of black and white?
Your life can still be everything that you were dreaming of.
Just take a look around you and see all the colors of love.
You wake up every morning and go through the same old grind.
You don't know how the light at the window could be so unkind.
If blue is the color that you choose when the road is rough,
you know you really need to believe in the colors of love.

(CHORUS)
The colors of love
are as beautiful as a rainbow.
The colors of love
shine on everyone in the world.

Are negative thoughts and emotions painful to express?
They're just tiny drops in the ocean of happiness.
And these are the feelings you must learn to rise above.
Your whole life is a picture you paint with the colors of love.

(CHORUS)

To Each His Own [Unit 8]

He doesn't care for Dali.
The colors are too bright.
He says that Picasso
got everything just right.
She can't stand the movies
that are filmed in Hollywood.
She likes Almodóvar.
She thinks he's really good.
He's inspired by everything
she thinks is second-rate.
She's moved and fascinated
by the things he loves to hate.
He's crazy about art that only
turns her heart to stone.
I guess that's why they say
to each his own.
He likes pencil drawings.
She prefers photographs.
He takes her to the art museum,
but she just laughs and laughs.
He loves the Da Vinci
that's hanging by the door.
She prefers the modern art
that's lying on the floor.
"No kidding! You'll love it. Just wait and see.
It's perfect in every way."
She shakes her head. "It's not for me.
It's much too old and gray."
She thinks he has the worst taste
that the world has ever known.
I guess that's why they say
to each his own.
But when it's time to say good-bye,
they both feel so alone.
I guess that's why they say
to each his own.

Workbook

Joan Saslow ■ Allen Ascher

with Terra Brockman

PEARSON
Longman

UNIT 6

Eating Well

TOPIC PREVIEW

1 **Look at the food pyramid. Write T (true), F (false), or NI (no information).**

1. The healthiest foods are at the top of the pyramid. ____

2. You should avoid vegetable oils at most meals. ____

3. Whole-grain bread is healthier than white bread. ____

4. Pasta is healthier than fruit. ____

5. You should eat more seafood than poultry. ____

6. Exercise is an important part of a healthy life. ____

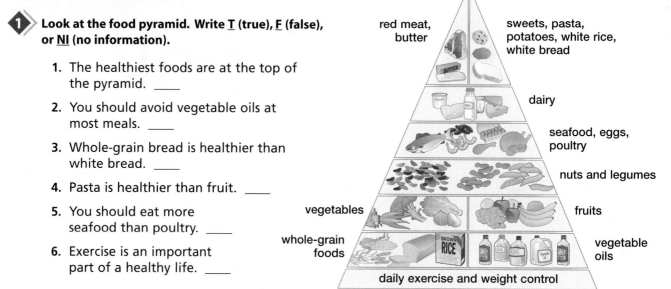

red meat, butter

sweets, pasta, potatoes, white rice, white bread

dairy

seafood, eggs, poultry

nuts and legumes

vegetables

fruits

whole-grain foods

vegetable oils

daily exercise and weight control

2 **Choose the correct response. Circle the letter.**

1. "Want to try some of the chocolate cookies?"

   a. No, thanks. I'm on a diet.   **b.** I used to. Not anymore.

2. "Why did you stop going to the gym?"

   a. Well, I would.   **b.** It was just too much trouble.

3. "Don't you usually drive to work?"

   a. Don't tell anyone.   **b.** I used to. Not anymore.

4. "What in the world are you doing?"

   a. Renting a car online.   **b.** I don't believe it.

5. "Aren't you on a diet?"

   a. Yes, you only live once!   **b.** Yes, I am.

3 **WHAT ABOUT YOU?** Do you think you have healthy or unhealthy eating habits? What kinds of food do you eat? Use your <u>own</u> words.

LESSON 1

4 ▸ **Choose the correct response. Write the letter on the line.**

1. _____ "Please help yourself."

2. _____ "I'll pass on the chocolates."

3. _____ "I'm sorry. I didn't know you were on a diet."

4. _____ "Why don't we go for a walk after dinner?"

a. Good idea. Let's go!

b. Thanks. Everything smells so good.

c. Don't worry about it.

d. Don't you eat sweets?

5 ▸ **Complete the conversation. Use phrases from the box. Use each only once.**

is a vegetarian   is on a diet   is allergic to   doesn't care for   is avoiding

A: Let's have a dinner party Friday night. Help me prepare the menu.

B: OK. Remember that my sister _____,
1.

so we can't make anything too fatty. Why don't you make some chicken?

A: I would, but Stella _____.
2.

She never eats meat. Maybe I can make that rice dish.

B: I don't know. Miguel is trying to eat healthy,

whole-grain foods, so he _____ white rice these days.
3.

A: OK. . . . Then how about black bean soup with peppers?

B: Uh, I don't think Julio would like that. He _____ spicy food.
4.

A: Is there anything that everyone can eat?

B: Hmm . . . I don't know, but I hope you'll make that delicious chocolate cake for dessert!

A: I can't. Don't you remember how sick Paul was at our last dinner?

He _____ chocolate!
5.

B: Why don't we just go out to eat?

A: Good idea!

6 ▸ **WHAT ABOUT YOU? Fill in the blanks with a food item to make the sentences true for you.**

1. I eat too much / many _____.

2. I'm avoiding _____.

3. I don't care for _____.

4. I really like to eat _____.

5. _____ doesn't / don't agree with me.

7 Complete each negative <u>yes</u> / <u>no</u> question.

1. **A:** _Didn't you go to Latvia_____ last year?

   B: Yes, I did. I went to Latvia in August.

2. **A:** _____ meat?

   B: No, I don't. I never touch meat.

3. **A:** _____ a doctor?

   B: No, she's not. David's mother is a dentist.

4. **A:** _____ a wonderful play?

   B: Yes, it was terrific.

5. **A:** _____ some more noodles?

   B: No, thanks. I'm full. I've had enough.

6. **A:** _____ China before?

   B: Actually, no. I've been to Japan.

LESSON 2

8 Choose the correct response. Circle the letter.

1. "Have you tried the steak? It's delicious!"

   a. No, thanks. I'm a big meat eater.
   b. No, thanks. I can't stand steak.
   c. I used to, but now I'm a vegetarian.

2. "Are you a big coffee drinker?"

   a. The coffee's terrific!
   b. It's not a problem.
   c. Actually, I've been cutting back.

3. "I'm crazy about chocolate. What about you?"

   a. I'm a big chocolate eater.
   b. Yes, thank you.
   c. I don't care for coffee.

9 What do you think they are saying? Write sentences about these people and their food passions. Use the words and phrases from the box. Use each only once.

| ~~crazy about~~   don't care for   big ___ eater   love   addict   can't stand |

1. _I'm crazy about_
   asparagus.
   _____

2. _____
   _____
   _____

3. _____
   _____
   _____

4. _____
_____
_____

5. _____
_____
_____

6. _____
_____
_____

10 Read about Kate's food passions. Then complete each sentence with <u>used to</u> or <u>didn't use to</u> and the verb.

When I was a kid, I loved sweets. I think I ate about five cookies a day! When I was a teenager, I started eating a lot of meat. I had steaks and fries almost every day. I didn't care for vegetables or fruit. Then on my 20th birthday, I decided I needed a change, so I became a vegetarian. These days I eat meat again, but I avoid fatty foods and sugar. I've lost a lot of weight and I feel much better.

1. Kate _____ a lot of sweets, but now she avoids sugar.
(eat)

2. When she was a teenager, she _____ fatty foods.
(have)

3. Before she turned 20, she _____ vegetables.
(like)

4. She _____ a vegetarian, but now she eats meat.
(be)

5. Kate _____ care of herself, but now she eats well.
(take)

11 WHAT ABOUT YOU? Talk about your food passions and eating habits. Complete the paragraph. Use your <u>own</u> words.

I used to eat a lot of

LESSON 3

12 **Read the online article about healthy lifestyle changes. Then write T (true) or F (false) for each statement below, according to the article.**

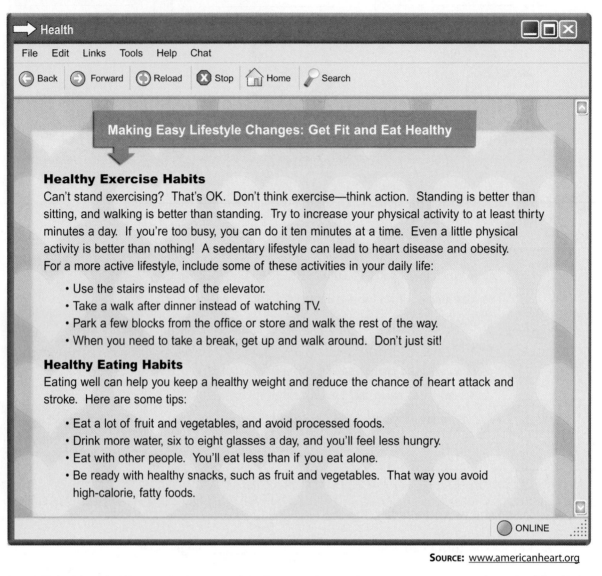

SOURCE: www.americanheart.org

_____ 1. Using the stairs doesn't count as exercise, so you should use the elevator whenever you can. It doesn't make any difference to your health anyway.

_____ 2. Snacks such as grapes and carrots that are low in calories are better than potato chips or chocolates.

_____ 3. When you eat by yourself, you'll probably eat less because it's boring when there's no one to enjoy and share the food with.

_____ 4. The chance of heart attack and stroke is the same for people who are fit and lead an active lifestyle and for people who are obese and lead a sedentary lifestyle.

_____ 5. The worst thing to do when you need a break is to get up and walk around. You only get more tired that way. You should sit down and relax.

_____ 6. Drinking a lot of water reduces the feeling of hunger, so you may end up eating less.

13 CHALLENGE. **Read the letter and then finish the advice column. Use your <u>own</u> words and ideas.**

Dear Health Advisor:

    I recently moved to a new city and got a new job. I have to sit at my desk all day, and then I sit at home and watch TV all evening. In the last four months, I have gained twenty pounds! I can't stand being overweight. What should I do?

Frank

Dear Frank:

    It sounds like you have made some negative lifestyle changes. Here are three easy, positive lifestyle changes you can start making today:

1. _____.

2. _____.

3. _____.

You'll feel much better!

LESSON 4

14 **Read the postcard. Fill in the blanks with the correct form of <u>taste</u>, <u>smell</u>, or <u>look</u>.**

Hi Reiko,

    I'm having a great time in Marrakech! Yesterday I walked in the main square, and it _____ like a scene from a movie!
1.
People in long, beautiful robes were everywhere, and there was so much food! I saw some fish that _____ like the kind we have
2.
at home. Somewhere else in the market, I couldn't see where, there was a kind of grilled meat that _____ terrific. I found it, but didn't know if I should try it.
3.
It _____ kind of strange, but I bought some anyway. It was delicious!
4.
It _____ both spicy and sweet. It wasn't at all what I expected!
5.
You should come here on your next vacation!

See you soon,

Junko

15 List some foods that go with the descriptions.

1. spicy _____
2. crunchy _____
3. sweet _____
4. sour _____
5. hard _____
6. chewy _____
7. salty _____

16 WHAT ABOUT YOU? Complete the paragraph. Describe an unusual food you have eaten. Where and when did you eat it? What did it look, smell, and taste like? Would you recommend it to someone or not?

One of the strangest things I've ever eaten is

GRAMMAR BOOSTER

A Fill in the blanks to make negative yes / no questions. Then use the information in parentheses to answer the questions with a short answer.

1. A: _____ you have a vegetarian friend?
   B: _____ .
   (None of my friends are vegetarian.)

2. A: _____ you trying to lose weight?
   B: _____ .
   (I'm on a diet.)

3. A: _____ he like spicy food?
   B: _____ .
   (He hates spicy food.)

4. A: _____ there sardines on that pizza?
   B: _____ .
   (The pizza has sardines on it.)

5. A: _____ Sandra allergic to fish?
   B: _____ .
   (She doesn't have any problem eating fish.)

B Complete each conversation with a suggestion, using Why don't or Why doesn't.

1. A: I'm too tired to cook dinner tonight.
   B: *Why don't we* _____ go out to eat?

2. A: Fred's old van keeps breaking down.
   B: _____ buy a new car?

3. A: My mother thinks the hotel room will be too small.
   B: _____ reserve a suite?

4. A: That film was really long and boring!
   B: _____ watch a short comedy next time?

Read the statement and then answer the question, using an appropriate form of <u>used to</u> for each of the following.

1. "Since Charlie started going to the gym every day, he's lost so much weight."

   Did Charlie use to go to the gym every day?

   _No, he didn't use to go to the gym every day_____.

2. "Now that he has more time, Scott has started making dinner every night."

   Did Scott use to make dinner every night?

   _____.

3. "Paul began getting up early every day when he had children."

   Did Paul use to get up early every day before he had children?

   _____.

4. "As Cindy got older, her tastes changed, and now she actually likes eating vegetables."

   Did Cindy use to like eating vegetables?

   _____.

5. "I can't believe Judy has become a vegetarian!"

   Did Judy use to eat meat?

   _____.

6. "When Peter's doctor told him that he had better stop smoking, he quit."

   Did Peter use to smoke?

   _____.

7. "Soon after Pamela and Ed got married, they bought their first house."

   Did Pamela and Ed use to have a house before they got married?

   _____.

D **Write a <u>yes</u> / <u>no</u> question for each response, using a form of <u>used to</u>.**

1. A: _Did you use to work in that part of the city_____?

   B: Yes, I did. I used to work in that part of the city a few years ago.

2. A: _____?

   B: No, they didn't. People didn't use to watch DVDs for entertainment.

3. A: _____?

   B: Yes, it did. Eating used to be simpler.

4. A: _____?

   B: No, they didn't. Foods didn't use to have labels.

5. A: _____?

   B: Yes, I did. I used to live closer to work.

6. A: _____?

   B: Yes, they did. Cars used to use a lot more gas.

JUST FOR FUN

1 Read the clues and complete the crossword puzzle.

Across

4. It's a long, green (or white) vegetable.

6. They are white and yellow inside, and they come from a chicken.

8. It's raw fish on rice.

9. They're made from cocoa beans. People often give them in a box as a gift.

Down

1. It's made of milk, it's sweet, and it comes in many flavors.

2. It's made with soybeans and is popular in Asia and with vegetarians all over the world.

3. These are small fish that are usually very salty.

5. This is a little like fish but comes in a shell. Some people are allergic to this.

7. Vegetarians never eat this.

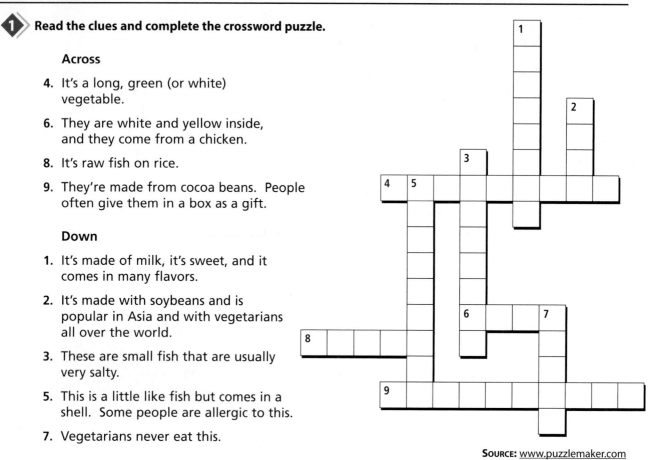

SOURCE: www.puzzlemaker.com

2 BRAINTEASER. Look at the picture and then read the clues. Write the name on the line.

1. _____
2. _____
3. _____
4. _____
5. _____

Clues:
- Patty doesn't care for vegetables.
- Al's allergic to dairy products.
- Fish doesn't agree with Greg.
- Marcia is a vegetarian.
- Nicolas is trying to lose weight.

Psychology and Personality

TOPIC PREVIEW

1 Look at the color tests and the pictures of the two women. Based on the
answers to the tests and the results, who do you think is Michelle and who
do you think is Janet? Label the pictures.

COLOR TEST   Name: <u>Michelle Duval</u>

1) Which color do you prefer for shoes?
   - ☑ black   ◯ white
   - ◯ light brown   ◯ red

2) Which color of clothes do you prefer
   to wear?
   - ◯ green   ☑ gray
   - ◯ white   ◯ pink

3) Which color makes you feel sad?
   - ◯ white   ◯ dark blue
   - ◯ silver   ☑ orange

4) What color would you paint your
   bedroom?
   - ◯ gold   ◯ purple
   - ☑ dark gray   ◯ green

5) Which color do you think is the most
   relaxing?
   - ☑ purple   ◯ yellow
   - ◯ green   ◯ blue

RESULT

According to your answers, you
probably keep your feelings inside
most of the time. You often feel sad
and down.

---

1. _____

2. _____

COLOR TEST   Name: <u>Janet Gamble</u>

1) Which color do you prefer for shoes?
   - ◯ black   ◯ white
   - ◯ light brown   ☑ red

2) Which color of clothes do you prefer
   to wear?
   - ◯ green   ◯ gray
   - ◯ white   ☑ pink

3) Which color makes you feel sad?
   - ◯ white   ☑ dark blue
   - ◯ silver   ◯ orange

4) What color would you paint your
   bedroom?
   - ☑ gold   ◯ purple
   - ◯ dark gray   ◯ green

5) Which color do you think is the most
   relaxing?
   - ◯ purple   ☑ yellow
   - ◯ green   ◯ blue

RESULT

According to your answers, you
probably don't have any problems
expressing your feelings. You are
always cheerful and happy.

---

2 WHAT ABOUT YOU? Fill in the chart. Which color makes you feel . . .

happy? _____

lucky? _____

calm? _____

powerful? _____

down in the dumps? _____

FACTOID: Men, women, and colors
Studies have found that women
prefer red over blue, but men prefer
blue over red.

SOURCE: <u>www.colormatters.com</u>

3 ▶ **Choose the sentence that has a similar meaning. Circle the letter.**

1. I just feel a little out of sorts.

   a. I am just kind of busy.

   b. I don't feel quite right.

2. Nothing I can put my finger on.

   a. It's not anything exactly.

   b. I don't need anything to eat.

3. Michael's been feeling a bit blue lately.

   a. Michael's been a little sad lately.

   b. Michael's been feeling quite great lately.

4. Maybe a good comedy would cheer you up.

   a. Maybe you shouldn't see a good comedy.

   b. Maybe a good comedy would make you feel better.

LESSON 1

4 ▶ **Put the conversation in order. Write the number on the line.**

_1_ Dad, can I paint my bedroom?

____ It's depressing.

____ How about red or black?

____ Why? What's wrong with black?

____ Well, red's OK, but black is out of the question.

____ Sure. What color?

_7_ To me, black is calm, not depressing.

> **FACTOID: Olympic Colors**
>
> The official Olympic logo was created by Baron Pierre de Coubertin in 1913. It consists of five interlacing rings of blue, yellow, black, green, and red. At least one of these colors is found in the flag of every nation.
>
> **SOURCE:** www.colormatters.com

5 ▶ **CHALLENGE. Complete Lucia's letter. Use gerunds and infinitives. Remember to put the verbs in the correct tense.**

Hi Rebecca:

Well, I finally made a change! Last week I said to myself, "I _____ at our old
                                                              1. can't stand / look

kitchen walls one more day!" So I _____ them! My roommate Sara said we
                                    2. decide / repaint

should _____ a plan before we do it. She even _____
        3. discuss / make   **4. suggest / take**

a month or two to think about it. She said we should _____ first, but I already
                                                      5. practice / paint

know how to paint. I don't _____. Anyway, I _____ new things.
                            6. need / learn   **7. not mind / try**

Finally, we _____ the kitchen a cheerful color—bright yellow! I'm not sure, but
            8. choose / give

Sara _____ the new color. In fact, I don't think she _____!
     9. not seem / like   **10. enjoy / paint**

But I hope she does, because I _____ the living room next. I _____
                               11. plan / paint   **12. would like / paint**

it fuchsia! What do you think about that?

Lucia

6 Complete each sentence with a word from the box. Use each word only once.

depressing	calm	exciting	cheerful	disgusting	nervous

1. I hate this theater. The lobby always smells terrible, and the bathrooms are dirty and

_____.

2. Don't get _____ when you hear the fire alarm. Be sure to stay _____.

3. Last night's ball game was so _____! Our team won the championship!

4. Penny is such a(n) _____ person. She always gives you a big smile when she

sees you.

5. I don't feel like watching that film. I hear it's very _____. I'm not in the mood

for a sad movie.

LESSON 2

7 Complete the conversation. Use the correct preposition with the verb or adjective, and a gerund.

A: You look a little blue. What's up?

B: Oh, nothing really. I'm just _tired of working_ late every night.

1. tired / work

A: Is that all? You really look down.

B: I'm _____ the same thing every day. And I also feel

2. bored / do

_____ too little time at home.

3. sad / spend

A: Have you _____ overtime?

4. complained / work

B: No. I'm _____ my boss angry. I had to _____ a

5. afraid / make   6. apologize / finish

report late. And now my boss is _____ us more work.

7. talking / give

A: Wow! I see why you are feeling blue. Why don't you start looking for a new job?

8 Suggest something to cheer these people up. Write complete sentences.

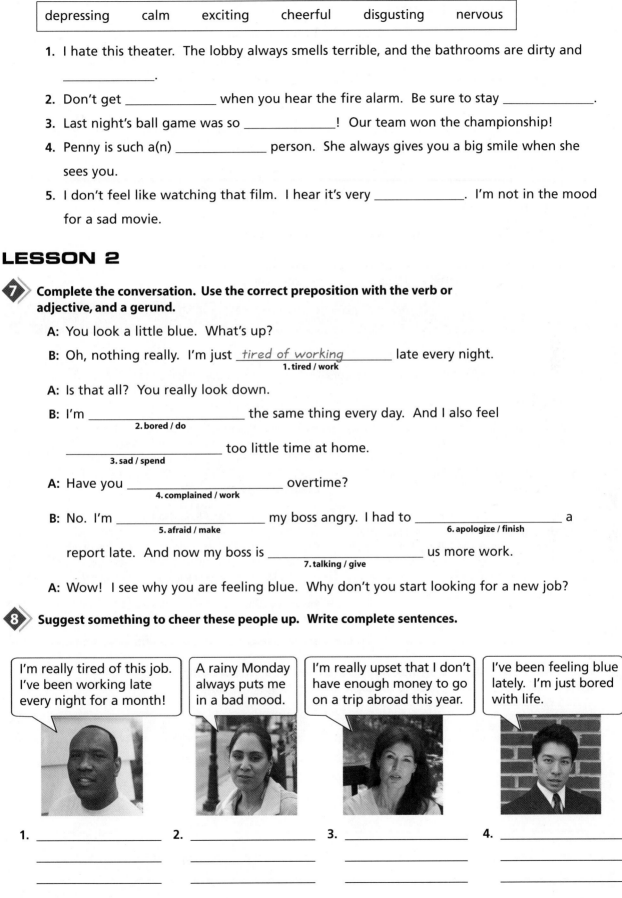

I'm really tired of this job. I've been working late every night for a month!

A rainy Monday always puts me in a bad mood.

I'm really upset that I don't have enough money to go on a trip abroad this year.

I've been feeling blue lately. I'm just bored with life.

1. _____
   _____
   _____

2. _____
   _____
   _____

3. _____
   _____
   _____

4. _____
   _____
   _____

LESSON 3

9 ▸ **Complete each sentence. Circle the letter.**

1. He's got a great ____. I just love spending time with him!

   a. personality   **b.** nurture   **c.** genetics

2. When I need to think, I prefer to be alone with my ____.

   a. genetics   **b.** nature   **c.** thoughts

3. Some people believe that your personality comes from your ____, that is, your friends, your experiences, and everything around you.

   a. nature   **b.** thoughts   **c.** environment

4. I believe personality has nothing to do with one's home or friends, but more to do with ____ —traits that come from one's parents.

   a. emotions   **b.** genetics   **c.** thoughts

10 ▸ **Read the web postings on <u>YourPersonality.com</u>. Rank the people from 1 to 5, 1 being the most introverted and 5 being the most extroverted.**

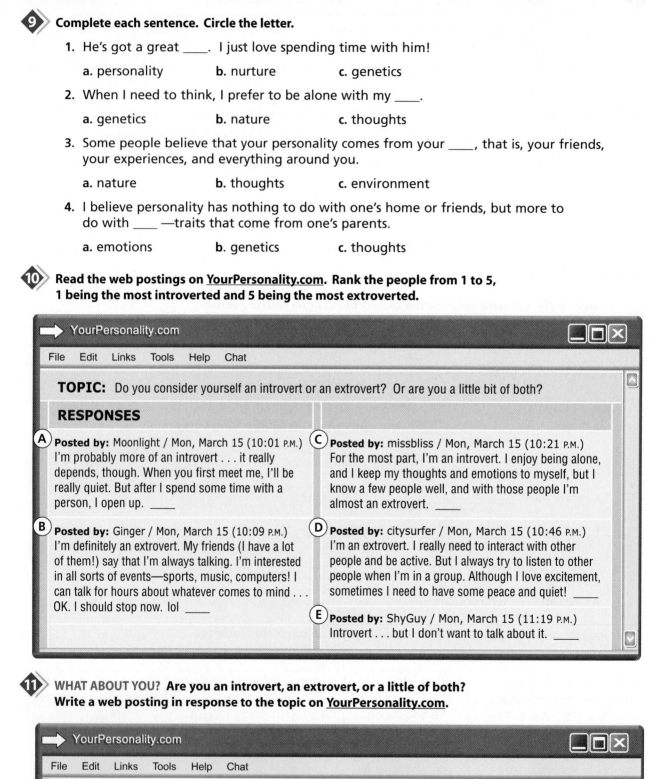

11 ▸ **WHAT ABOUT YOU? Are you an introvert, an extrovert, or a little of both? Write a web posting in response to the topic on <u>YourPersonality.com</u>.**

LESSON 4

 Read the article and answer the questions below.

ASTROLOGY – FINDING YOUR PERSONALITY IN THE STARS

Why do you think and act the way you do? What is the secret to your thoughts and emotions? Why do you have the personality you do? Is it nature or nurture? Genetics or the environment? Or could it be the sun and the stars?

Some people think that birth order influences personality, but many others believe that the day you were born on influences your personality. These people believe in astrology. They believe that the sun and the stars influence human personality and events.

Astrology may be a way to understand human personality. Or it may be a false science. But millions of people around the world read their astrological horoscope every day—just in case!

Aquarius ≈
Jan 20–Feb 18
- very active
- cheerful
- can be a clown

Pisces)(
Feb 19–Mar 20
- honest
- easily bored with jobs
- likes quiet time

Aries ♈
Mar 21–Apr 19
- enjoys being alone
- hard to get to know
- keeps thoughts and emotions inside

Taurus ♉
Apr 20–May 20
- calm
- seeks peace
- good listener

Gemini ♊
May 21–Jun 21
- worries about things
- can be self-critical
- can be hard to know

 Cancer ♋
Jun 22–Jul 22
- interested in travel
- enjoys being with other people
- always behaves appropriately

Leo ♌
Jul 23–Aug 22
- happy with lots of people
- cheers people up
- crazy about nature

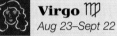 **Virgo** ♍
Aug 23–Sept 22
- keeps ideas inside
- likes to spend time alone
- enjoys reading

Libra ♎
Sept 23–Oct 23
- conservative
- spends time with a few friends
- has strong emotions

Scorpio ♏
Oct 24–Nov 21
- friendly
- sensitive to others' emotions
- not easy to get to know

Sagittarius ♐
Nov 22–Dec 21
- creative
- likes everything in moderation
- gets along with everyone

Capricorn ♑
Dec 22–Jan 19
- has a lot of friends
- interested in events
- loves excitement

1. What is the basic idea behind astrology? _____
   _____.

2. Which of the zodiac signs describe more of an introvert? _____.

3. Which signs describe more of an extrovert? _____.

4. What sign of the zodiac are you? _____ Does the description for your sign
   describe you? Why or why not? _____
   _____.

GRAMMAR BOOSTER

A Complete each sentence. Circle the letter.

1. I love ____ TV in the evening.
   a. watch   **b.** to watch   **c.** watched

2. I hurt my knee last month, so I quit ____.
   a. jog   **b.** to jog   **c.** jogging

3. ____ too many sweets is bad for you.
   a. Eating   **b.** Eat   **c.** Eaten

4. My favorite thing to do after work is ____ magazines.
   a. read   **b.** to reading   **c.** to read

5. If you get an early start, you'll have a better chance of ____ your work on time.
   a. finish   **b.** finishing   **c.** to finish

6. Do you mind my ____ the window? It's freezing in here!
   a. closing   **b.** close   **c.** closed

7. ____ opera well is a hard thing to do.
   a. Sing   **b.** To sing   **c.** To singing

B Complete each sentence with a gerund or an infinitive. Use verbs from the box.
Use each verb only once.

| cook   play   study   do   watch   ride |

1. Susan can't stand _____ the dishes after dinner.

2. Michael loves _____ the guitar.

3. Marianna hates _____ for exams.

4. Joseph would like _____ his bike.

5. Beth doesn't mind _____ for her family.

6. Jim likes _____ TV.

C Find and correct six errors in the diary.

Usually I don't mind studying, but last night I was so sick of do homework that I decided

to go out with Amy. She felt like go to the movies, so I suggested to go to a romantic comedy.

But Amy said she hates romantic movies and suggested watch an action movie instead. But I

can't stand so much violence, so finally we chose seeing that new Japanese animated film.

We both really enjoyed to watch it, and we had a wonderful time.

D **Unscramble the words and phrases to complete the conversations.**
Use a gerund or an infinitive.

1. **A:** *John can't stand thinking about graduation* _____.
      think / John / about / can't stand / graduation

   B: I know. _____.
      He / leave / hates / his friends

2. **A:** _____.
      refuse / dinner / tonight / I / make

   B: Fine by me. _____.
      don't mind / go / I / out to eat

3. **A:** _____?
      buy / discussed / Have / you and Peter / a house

   B: Yes. _____.
      find / We / would like / something bigger

4. **A:** _____.
      tonight / you / I / see / didn't expect

   B: Well, _____.
      at the last minute / I / decided / come

E **Complete each sentence with an affirmative or negative gerund.**

1. You should start _____ every day if you want to lose weight.
      exercise

2. Sue was worried about _____ enough money to pay her bills.
      have

3. When will you finish _____ on that project?
      work

4. Avoid _____ a cell phone while you're driving.
      use

5. Stella and I have considered _____ a new car. We just don't have the money.
      buy

6. I apologize for _____ you that I'd be late. I'm sorry that you've waited so long.
      tell

7. Jeff really dislikes _____ to strangers. He's such an introvert!
      talk

8. A good way to learn English is to practice _____ a diary in English.
      write

9. I believe in _____ fatty foods. You'll be healthier.
      eat

JUST FOR FUN

1 Unscramble the letters to form words.

1. (TTROERVEX)   E X __ __ __ __ __ __
2. (SONTYERPALI)   P __ __ __ __ __ __ __ __ __
3. (TURUREN)   N __ __ __ __ __ __
4. (NOTIOEM)   E __ __ __ __ __ __
5. (MRAGINHC)   C H __ __ __ __ __ __
6. (BIILSNG)   S __ __ __ __ __ __

2 Choose the best word from the box to describe each person. Write the word under the picture.

| creative | self-critical | rebel | introvert | clown | conservative |

1. _____

2. _____

3. _____

4. _____

5. _____

6. _____

3 **FIGURE IT OUT!** Here are the names of four colors with the vowels removed. What are the four colors?

PLTNM   MV   FCHS   CRM

Answers to Exercise 3: PLATINUM, MAUVE, FUCHSIA, CREAM

Enjoying the Arts

TOPIC PREVIEW

1 Look at the two paintings and read the conversation.

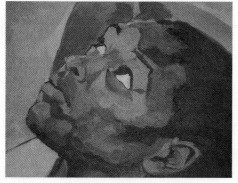

Serena by Jessica Miller-Smith, U.S.A (2000)

Gerald: This painting is really weird. Is that by Jessica Miller-Smith?

Sophie: Yes. It says it was painted in 2000.

Gerald: I don't like it. It makes me feel nervous. What do you think?

Sophie: I think it's pretty cool. I find it exciting. It would look fantastic in my bedroom.

Gerald: Ugh! I'd rather look at a plain wall.

Thoughts by Agnes Geniusaite, Lithuania (1997)

Gerald: Hey, look at this incredible painting! It says it's by Agnes Geniusaite. I'm just crazy about her stuff.

Sophie: I think it's sort of depressing.

Gerald: Really? Maybe you're just feeling a little blue today.

Sophie: Maybe. But I don't care for it at all. I'm not that crazy about dark colors.

Gerald: Well, to each his own.

Now check the statements that are true.

☐ **1.** Gerald thinks Jessica Miller-Smith is pretty cool.

☐ **2.** Sophie likes Miller-Smith.

☐ **3.** Gerald likes Agnes Geniusaite's art.

☐ **4.** Sophie finds Geniusaite's painting depressing.

☐ **5.** Sophie prefers darker colors to brighter colors.

☐ **6.** Sophie and Gerald like the same kind of art.

2 Write a plus (+) next to the statements that indicate that the person likes the art, and a minus (−) next to the statements that indicate that the person doesn't like it.

_____ **1.** I'd rather look at a plain wall.

_____ **2.** Her photographs are wonderful.

_____ **3.** It's an unforgettable film.

_____ **4.** Don't you think Vera Wang's fashions are gorgeous?

_____ **5.** Actually, I find them kind of boring.

_____ **6.** To tell you the truth, I'm not too crazy about it.

_____ **7.** Oh, I'm really into it!

_____ **8.** I used to be into photography, but not now.

3 Choose the correct response. Circle the letter.

1. "We should buy this painting. It would look great in our living room!"

   a. What do you think?   b. I'd rather look at a plain wall.   c. I used to be into films.

2. "Don't you find this painting a little too dark?"

   a. Well, to each his own.   b. No. I like bright colors.   c. No. I think it's just right.

3. "I think Anne Klein's fashions are fantastic. What about you?"

   a. Is it a Picasso?   b. I find them boring.   c. They were painted in 1903.

4. "Just look at the colors in this photograph. Aren't they amazing?"

   a. This sculpture is sort of interesting.   b. Maybe you're just feeling blue today.   c. Honestly, I'm not crazy about really bright colors.

5. "That film is really weird. I don't think anyone cares for it at all."

   a. I kind of like it, actually.   b. Is it a drawing?   c. It would look nice over my desk.

4 WHAT ABOUT YOU? What do <u>you</u> think of the paintings in Exercise 1? Fill in the chart.

	Miller-Smith	Geniusaite
What do you like about it?		
What do you dislike about it?		
Where would you hang it?		

LESSON 1

5 Read a page from a tour guide about Paris. Make a recommendation to someone who is visiting Paris. Complete the conversation, using the information in the tour guide.

The Rodin Museum

There are many wonderful museums to see while you are visiting Paris. One museum you should be sure to visit is the lovely Rodin Museum. The Rodin Museum houses over 6,600 sculptures. There is also an impressive garden. A large number of sculptures are presented in this setting, including Rodin's most famous work, *The Thinker*. In addition to the sculptures, take a look at the excellent drawing collection. Many of Rodin's sketches are there.

SOURCE: www.musee-rodin.fr

YOU Be sure _____ 1.

in Paris.

B: Really? Why's that?

YOU Well, _____ 2. .

B: No kidding!

YOU They also _____ 3. .

You'll _____ 4. .

B: Thanks for the recommendation.

6 Read each sentence and decide if it's in the active voice (**A**) or passive voice (**P**).

1. Many people visit the Metropolitan Museum of Art in New York. ____

2. The glass pyramid in front of the Louvre was finished in 1989. ____

3. A color poster of the painting was made available. ____

4. The museum catalog has been translated into many languages. ____

5. Akira Kurosawa directed the film *Seven Samurai* in 1954. ____

6. That vase was made in ancient Egypt. ____

7. The photograph was taken fifty years ago. ____

8. Matisse painted *La Musique* in 1910. ____

7 CHALLENGE. Use the information in the chart to write two sentences. Write the first sentence in the active voice and the second one in the passive voice. Be sure to use the correct verb with the artwork.

Art Object	Artist	Year
1. *Still Life with Watermelon* (painting)	Pablo Picasso	1946
2. *Vines and Olive Trees* (painting)	Joan Miró	1919
3. *The Raven and the First Men* (wood figure)	Bill Reid	1994
4. *A. I.* (film)	Steven Spielberg	2002
5. *Waterfront Demonstration* (photograph)	Dorothea Lange	1934

1. Active: *Pablo Picasso painted "Still Life with Watermelon" in 1946* _____.

   Passive: *"Still Life with Watermelon" was painted by Pablo Picasso in 1946* _____.

2. Active: _____.

   Passive: _____.

3. Active: _____.

   Passive: _____.

4. Active: _____.

   Passive: _____.

5. Active: _____.

   Passive: _____.

LESSON 2

8 Choose the correct response. Write the letter on the line.

1. ____ "Is this vase handmade?"

2. ____ "What do you think of this painting?"

3. ____ "Where was the figure made?"

4. ____ "Do you know when this photograph was taken?"

5. ____ "What's the bowl made of?"

a. Clay. It's handmade.

b. Yes, it is.

c. It says it was made in Bulgaria.

d. Not much. I'm not too crazy about the colors.

e. Around 1980, I think.

9 Find a word in each row that describes each picture. Write sentences about the pictures, using the words. You will use some words more than once.

Material	cloth	glass	wood	stone	clay	gold
Object	bowl	figure	vase	bag		
Adjective	simple gorgeous	weird wonderful	beautiful boring	fantastic cheerful	lovely interesting	depressing cool

1. *The figure is made of wood.*
   It's interesting.

2. _____
   _____

3. _____
   _____

4. _____
   _____

5. _____
   _____

6. _____
   _____

10 Use the words below to write questions about the items. Then complete the answers to the questions. Use contractions when possible.

1. **A:** *What's the vase made of* _____?
   <u>what / vase / made of</u>

   B: It _'s_ made of stone.

2. **A:** _____?
   <u>where / dolls / made</u>

   B: They _____ in Thailand.

3. **A:** _____?
   <u>statue / carved / by the Chinese</u>

   B: No, it _____ by the Vietnamese.

4. **A:** _____?
   <u>what / guitar / used for</u>

   B: It _____ special festivals.

5. **A:** _____?
   <u>how / chair / built</u>

   B: It _____ by hand.

6. **A:** _____?
   <u>robe / worn / in Japan</u>

   B: Yes, _____.

LESSON 3

 11 Read the advice column from *ArtNews*. Then rewrite each false statement as a true statement.

ArtNews Ask Alice—Advice for New Artists

Dear Alice,

I saw my first Matisse painting when I was five years old. Since then, I have wanted to be a famous artist. I began studying art seriously five years ago and now I want to go to art school in Paris. Art is the one great love of my life. But my family doesn't know much about art. They have some art at home, of course, but they never go to museums. I go to museums almost every week. My family thinks I'm crazy. Am I?

Donald

Dear Donald,

It is wonderful that you are fascinated by art. But Paris is an expensive city and far away. Maybe you should go to an art school closer to your home. You will find it exciting to be around students who also love art. And who knows . . . maybe your family will become interested in art, too. Good luck!

Alice

1. Donald thinks his family is crazy. _____ .

2. His family knows a lot about art. _____ .

3. Donald saw his first Matisse painting five years ago. _____
_____ .

4. He has been studying art since he was five years old. _____
_____ .

5. Alice thinks Donald should go to art school in Paris. _____
_____ .

12 WHAT ABOUT YOU? **Check the boxes that describe how Donald, his family, and you feel about art.**

	Donald	His family	You
love(s) art	✔		
collect(s) art			
doesn't / don't care about art			
make(s) art			
want(s) to be an artist			
is / are crazy about art			
has / have artistic talent			
visit(s) art museums often			
has / have art at home			

13 WHAT ABOUT YOU? **How does art fit into your life? Use the phrases in the chart in Exercise 12 to write a short paragraph about yourself.**

LESSON 4

14 Complete this biography of Pablo Picasso, using the passive voice.

Pablo Ruiz Picasso began studying art with his father. Then from 1895 until 1904, he painted in Barcelona. During this time, he made his first trip to Paris, where he _____
1. inspire
by the artwork of Henri de Toulouse-Lautrec.

In Paris, Picasso _____
2. influence
by all the poverty he saw. He was sad and angry that so many people lived without enough food or clothing. He painted many pictures of poor people to bring attention to their situation.

In 1906, Picasso met the artist Henri Matisse, who was to become his longtime friend. Picasso _____ in Matisse's style,
3. interest
but he did not imitate it. The artists he really admired were Georges Braque and Joan Miró. Picasso _____ by Braque's and
4. fascinate
Miró's work. Together the three artists started the movement known as Cubism.

One of Picasso's most famous artistic pieces is *Guernica*. Picasso _____ by the violence of
5. move
the Spanish Civil War. This prompted him to paint the piece.

15 CHALLENGE. Read the biography in Exercise 14 again. Rewrite the sentences, changing them from the passive voice to the active voice.

1. _The artwork of Henri de Toulouse-Lautrec inspired Picasso_ .

2. _____ .

3. _____ .

4. _____ .

5. _____ .

16 WHAT ABOUT YOU? Write a paragraph about your favorite kind of art and your favorite artist. Use some of the phrases from the box.

| interested in | fascinated by | inspired by | moved by | influenced by |

I'm a big fan of _____. _____ is my

favorite _____.

GRAMMAR
BOOSTER

A ▸ **Complete each sentence. Circle the letter.**

1. This vase _____ made in 1569.

   a. is   **b.** has   **c.** was   **d.** were

2. Coffee is _____ in Colombia.

   a. grow   **b.** grew   **c.** grown   **d.** been growing

3. Business cards _____ exchanged at the meeting.

   a. is   **b.** being   **c.** was   **d.** were

4. The art exhibition was _____ by over 1,000 people.

   a. attending   **b.** attended   **c.** attend   **d.** will attend

5. I _____ invited, but I went anyway.

   a. wasn't   **b.** hasn't   **c.** isn't   **d.** weren't

B ▸ **Write sentences in the passive voice, using the verbs in parentheses. Use the correct verb tenses.**

1. French (speak) in Quebec, Canada. _____.

2. The Taj Mahal (build) around 1631. _____.

3. A new art museum (open) next year. _____.

4. These CDs (make) in Korea. _____.

5. "Let it Be" (write) by John Lennon. _____.

6. Your DVD player (repair) now. _____.

7. *Cornflowers* (paint) in 1876. _____.

8. The *Mona Lisa* (see) by millions of people since it was painted in the 16th century.

   _____.

C ▸ **Read this description of a museum. Find and correct five mistakes in the use of the passive voice. The first mistake is already corrected.**

The Frick Collection

                                     was built

The mansion of Henry Clay Frick ~~builded~~ in 1914 at the corner of Fifth Avenue and
                              ^

East 70th Street in New York City. It later opened to the public. Several improvements

have made over the years. Works of Monet, El Greco, Bernini, Degas, Vermeer, and

many other artists found throughout the mansion. Some of the museum's large

collection of art is display at temporary exhibitions around the world.

D Rewrite the sentences in the passive voice. Use a <u>by</u> phrase only if it is important or necessary to know who or what is performing the action.

1. People in China made this DVD player.

   This DVD player was made in China _____.

2. Artists hand painted these plates in France.

   _____.

3. They make good cars in Japan and Korea.

   _____.

4. They sell Brazilian coffee all over the world.

   _____.

5. Swiss companies still make most of the world's best watches.

   _____.

6. Shakespeare wrote *King Lear*.

   _____.

E Rewrite the sentences in the passive voice in Exercise D as <u>yes</u> / <u>no</u> questions.

1. *Was this DVD player made in China* _____ ?
2. _____ ?
3. _____ ?
4. _____ ?
5. _____ ?
6. _____ ?

JUST FOR FUN

1 Unscramble the letters to find what material each object is made of. Then match the item with the picture.

____ 1. r e l v i s _____ earrings

____ 2. y a l c _____ vase

____ 3. s a l g s _____ vase

____ 4. c h o t l _____ doll

____ 5. n e s t o _____ bowl

____ 6. d o o w _____ figure

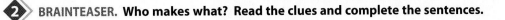

2 BRAINTEASER. **Who makes what? Read the clues and complete the sentences.**

1. The figure was sculpted by _____.

2. The photograph was taken by _____.

3. The suit was designed by _____.

4. The painting was done by _____.

5. The pottery was made by _____.

Clues:

Leo takes a lot of pictures.

Nicole works in the fashion industry.

Ju works with stone.

Brigitte's exhibit is at the gallery.

Jean uses clay in his work.

"Art washes away from the soul the dust of everyday life." – Pablo Picasso

Living with Computers

TOPIC PREVIEW

1 Read the four people's situations. What electronic items do you think they may need? Choose the items from the box and write them on the lines.

digital camera	cell phone	speaker	headset	PDA	CD drive
laptop	camcorder	printer	joystick	scanner	MP3 player

1. Tom is traveling to Europe. He wants to take a lot of pictures but doesn't want to bring a lot of film with him. He also wants to make a home video of his trip.

   _____ _____

   _____ _____

2. Mike is preparing for a speech for twenty people. He wants to give each person in the audience a copy of his five-page report. He also wants to add some photos to the report. His report is saved in his computer.

   _____ _____

   _____ _____

3. Gerry is very busy and has a lot of meetings in different cities every week. She needs to organize and remember all the things she needs to do. She also has to be able to send e-mails and make phone calls when she's on the road or out of town.

   _____ _____

   _____ _____

4. Shannon spends three hours on the bus every day. She wants to listen to music that she likes on the bus, but she doesn't want to have to carry a lot of CDs.

   _____ _____

   _____ _____

2 Choose the correct response. Circle the letter.

1. "Did you just log on?"
   a. No, thanks.
   b. Yes. What are you up to?
   c. I'm still here.

2. "Am I interrupting you?"
   a. Great!
   b. Sorry about that.
   c. Not at all.

3. "What are you up to?"
   a. Just deleting e-mail.
   b. Photos of my trip.
   c. They're awesome.

4. "Are you still there?"
   a. I just logged on.
   b. I'm still here.
   c. Sorry about that.

3 WHAT ABOUT YOU? Check the correct box to show how often these things happen in your life.

	Every day	Sometimes	Not very often	Never
I get e-mail.	☐	☐	☐	☐
I log on to the Internet.	☐	☐	☐	☐
My printer won't print.	☐	☐	☐	☐
I get instant messages.	☐	☐	☐	☐
My computer crashes.	☐	☐	☐	☐

4 ▷ Look at the ads and complete the conversations with <u>as</u> . . . <u>as</u> and the appropriate adjective.

1. A: I'm thinking of getting a new computer game system.

B: Oh, yeah? What kind?

A: I've heard Giga-Game is a lot of fun.

B: Well, I think Game-Pro is just _as exciting as_ Giga-Game, but it's a lot cheaper.

A: Really? So, Game-Pro isn't nearly

_____ Giga-Game? I'll go check it out.

2. A: Did you get a new hard disk?

B: Yeah, my XZ 5400 crashed, and I had to replace it with the YZ 2500.

A: Are you satisfied with the new one? Is it very fast?

B: Well, to tell the truth, it's not nearly

_____ the old one!

3. A: Wow! Look at this! What do you think of the Monster Monitor? It's really big!

B: Well, yeah, but the 40-40 monitor is just

_____ the Monster.

4. A: I'm thinking of getting the C2000 digital camera. What do you think?

B: I've heard the C2000 isn't quite

_____ the Maxcam.

A: Really? Are you sure? I thought they were the same price.

5 CHALLENGE. **Look at the chart comparing two laptop computers. Complete the sentences, using (not) as . . . as and the adjective in parentheses. Use the adverbs almost, quite, just, and nearly.**

	Laptop-To-Go	Laptop-Friend	KEY
Weight	.5 kilograms	1.5 kilograms	**Better**
Ease of use	◑	◑	
Monitor screen quality	●	●	
Software package	◑	●	
Speed	◔	●	
Cost	$999	$1,099	**Worse**

1. The quality of the Laptop-To-Go's monitor is <u>*almost as good as*</u> the quality
   (good)
   of the Laptop-Friend's monitor.

2. Laptop-To-Go is _____ Laptop-Friend.
   (expensive)

3. Laptop-Friend is _____ Laptop-To-Go.
   (easy to use)

4. Laptop-To-Go is _____ Laptop-Friend.
   (fast)

5. The software package that comes with Laptop-To-Go is _____
   (good)
   the one that comes with Laptop-Friend.

6. Laptop-To-Go is _____ Laptop-Friend.
   (heavy)

6 WHAT ABOUT YOU? **Which laptop computer would you buy? Explain your reasons, using as . . . as and some of the adverbs from Exercise 5.**

LESSON 2

7 **Match each action with the correct purpose. Write the letter on the line.**

1. He enrolled in an electronics course
   because he ____.

2. She went to the electronics store
   because she ____.

3. I bought speakers because I ____.

4. He turned on the television because he ____.

5. She bought a palm pilot because she ____.

a. needed to buy a printer

b. needed to be more organized

c. wanted to learn how to repair computers

d. wanted to listen to music on the computer

e. wanted to watch the news

8 ⟩ **Rewrite the sentences in Exercise 7, using infinitives of purpose.**

1. _He enrolled in an electronics course to learn how to repair computers_____.

2. _____.

3. _____.

4. _____.

5. _____.

9 ⟩ **Use the icon prompts to complete the conversation.**

A: Could you take a look at this?

B: Sure. What's the problem?

A: Well, I clicked on the toolbar to _____ my document,
and now everything is gone!
1.

B: Don't worry. You probably accidentally clicked on the _____ icon.
2.
Just move your cursor over there and click on this icon to _____ it.
3.

A: Oh . . . there it is! Thank you!

10 ⟩ **Choose the best answer from the box to complete each sentence. Use each word or phrase only once.**

open	save	cut	paste	select	clicked on	toolbar	scroll down	print

1. Oh, no! I just lost all the work I've done on the document because I forgot to _____ the file.

2. You can't _____ if the printer is not turned on.

3. To _____ a word, move the cursor over the word and highlight it.

4. The warning tells you to delete the e-mail right away. Don't _____ it, or your computer may crash.

5. You don't have to type the entire paragraph again. Just copy and _____ it where you need it.

6. I _____ the icon and nothing happened. What did I do wrong?

7. The _____ has a list of icons that provide a quick way to use computer commands.

8. To see more information on the product, _____ to the bottom of the page.

9. Your article is great but a little too long. Could you _____ a few paragraphs?

Here's how some people use their computers. Look at the pictures and complete the sentences, using infinitives of purpose.

1. Ivana uses her computer *to join a chat room* .

2. Theresa uses the computer _____.

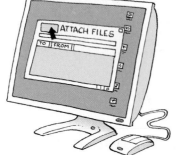

3. Edward uses his computer _____.

4. Frank uses his computer _____.

5. Liana uses her computer _____.

6. Martin uses his computer _____.

7. Abby uses the scanner _____ into the computer.

Read about how these people use the computer. Who is speaking? Choose one of the people from Exercise 11. Write the person's name under his or her picture.

I'm a fashion designer, and I really need to learn about what people wear and why they wear it. So I joined this chat room to talk with other people about fashion.

I have a lot of friends, and I like to keep in touch with them. So I send instant messages all the time.

I spend about eight hours a day surfing the Internet. I just love it. I guess you could say I'm a computer addict.

1. _Ivana_

2. _____

3. _____

I just graduated, so I created my own website to keep in touch with my classmates. It's been a lot of work. I used to surf the Internet all the time, but now I spend all my time creating and updating the website.

I'm a big music fan, so I've been using my computer to download music files. My friend just sent me a new song to download. Here . . . want to listen?

4. _____

5. _____

WHAT ABOUT YOU? Write a paragraph about how <u>you</u> use the computer. Be sure to answer these questions in your paragraph.

- How many hours do you use the computer each week?
- Do you use the computer more for work or for fun?
- Would you rather spend more time with people or with the computer?

LESSON 4

14 Read the online advice column. Then answer the questions.

→ Computer Safety   ◻◻✕

File   Edit   Links   Tools   Help   Chat

Keeping Your Computer Safe

These days, it only takes about twenty minutes on the Internet for your computer to get a virus. In fact, almost as soon as software recognizes and kills one computer virus, a new one appears. Here are some tips to help keep your computer secure.

1. Be careful with all e-mail messages.
If you receive an unexpected message, especially if it has an attachment, do not open it! Even if the message seems to come from your friends and family, be very careful about opening attachments. Computer viruses can get into your address book and use your friends' e-mail addresses. It may look like a message is coming from someone you know, when it is really coming from a virus.

2. Make your computer secure.
Go into your Internet Options and set your Privacy Protection to high. This will make it more difficult for someone to use your computer to send viruses.

3. Download AdAware.
This free software will let you know if anyone is tracking your Internet use. If they are, they might be sending your personal information, including credit card numbers, to someone who could use the information against you.

4. Download Virus Killer.
Virus Killer is another free software package you can download from the Internet. This software will kill many of the viruses that appear on your computer. It is a good way to make sure your computer is safe from viruses.

If you follow these simple tips, your computer should be safe. Good luck!

SOURCE: www.ncl.ac.uk

1. What can you do to prevent someone from using your computer to send viruses?

   _____.

2. Why does the article suggest downloading the two kinds of software?

   _____.

3. How can a virus use the address book in your computer?

   _____.

4. Why do you have to be careful about e-mails from people you know?

   _____.

15 WHAT ABOUT YOU? Write a paragraph about what you have done, or what you would like to do, to keep your computer safe.

A Look at the video game report cards. Write sentences comparing A-1 and Game Plan. Use the comparative form of the adjective or adverb in parentheses.

Video Game Reports — **A-1**

	0 ←→ 10
Sound quality	(5)
Visual quality	(8)
Interest level	(4)
Fun level	(6)
Violence level	(8)
Easy to play	(4)
Speed	(7)
Price	$89.95

Video Game Reports — **Game Plan**

	0 ←→ 10
Sound quality	(4)
Visual quality	(5)
Interest level	(8)
Fun level	(6)
Violence level	(7)
Easy to play	(7)
Speed	(4)
Price	$129.95

1. The A-1 sound quality is _better than the Game Plan sound quality_ .
   (good)

2. Game Plan is _____ .
   (interesting)

3. Game Plan is _____ .
   (violent)

4. Game Plan is _____ .
   (easy to play)

5. A-1 looks _____ .
   (good)

6. A-1 is _____ .
   (expensive)

7. A-1 runs _____ .
   (fast)

B Now look at the report card for a third video game. Write sentences comparing all three video games, using the superlative form of the adjective or adverb in parentheses.

Video Game Reports — **Top Game**

	0 ←→ 10
Sound quality	(8)
Visual quality	(8)
Interest level	(2)
Fun level	(2)
Violence level	(5)
Easy to play	(3)
Speed	(8)
Price	$199.95

1. _Top Game sound quality is the best_ .
   (good)

2. _____ .
   (expensive)

3. _____ .
   (fast)

4. _____ .
   (easy to play)

5. _____ .
   (interesting)

6. _____ .
   (violent)

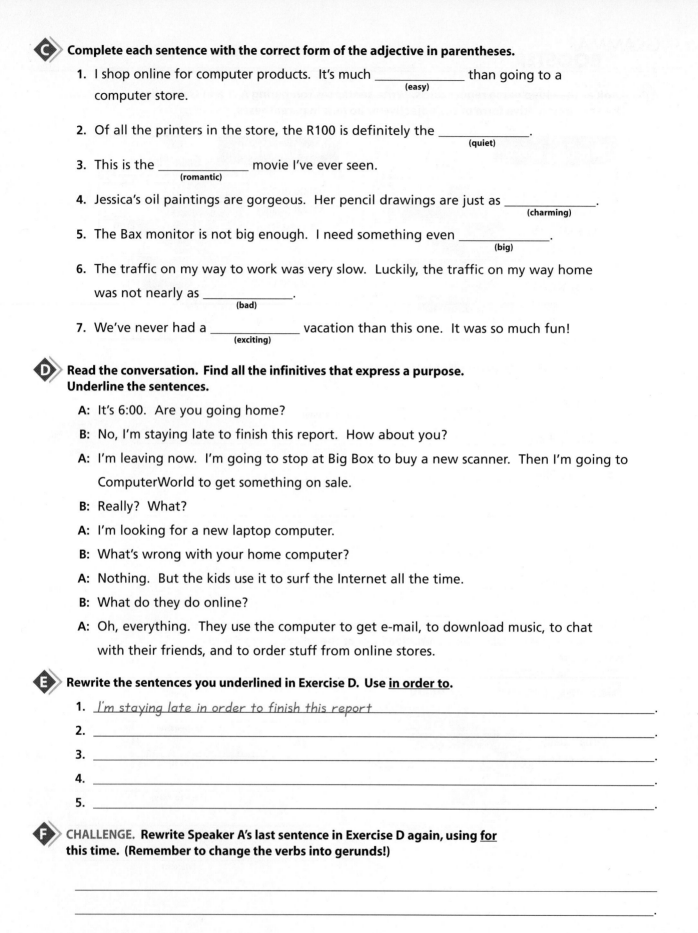

C ▷ Complete each sentence with the correct form of the adjective in parentheses.

1. I shop online for computer products. It's much _____ than going to a computer store.
   (easy)

2. Of all the printers in the store, the R100 is definitely the _____.
   (quiet)

3. This is the _____ movie I've ever seen.
   (romantic)

4. Jessica's oil paintings are gorgeous. Her pencil drawings are just as _____.
   (charming)

5. The Bax monitor is not big enough. I need something even _____.
   (big)

6. The traffic on my way to work was very slow. Luckily, the traffic on my way home was not nearly as _____.
   (bad)

7. We've never had a _____ vacation than this one. It was so much fun!
   (exciting)

D ▷ Read the conversation. Find all the infinitives that express a purpose. Underline the sentences.

A: It's 6:00. Are you going home?

B: No, I'm staying late to finish this report. How about you?

A: I'm leaving now. I'm going to stop at Big Box to buy a new scanner. Then I'm going to ComputerWorld to get something on sale.

B: Really? What?

A: I'm looking for a new laptop computer.

B: What's wrong with your home computer?

A: Nothing. But the kids use it to surf the Internet all the time.

B: What do they do online?

A: Oh, everything. They use the computer to get e-mail, to download music, to chat with their friends, and to order stuff from online stores.

E ▷ Rewrite the sentences you underlined in Exercise D. Use <u>in order to</u>.

1. *I'm staying late in order to finish this report* _____.

2. _____.

3. _____.

4. _____.

5. _____.

F ▷ CHALLENGE. Rewrite Speaker A's last sentence in Exercise D again, using <u>for</u> this time. (Remember to change the verbs into gerunds!)

_____

_____.

G Complete the sentences with <u>for</u> or <u>to</u>.

1. I like to shop online _____ delicious foods from Italy.

2. My son uses the computer _____ download music.

3. Judith e-mailed me _____ directions to the party.

4. Daniel uses the Internet _____ get the latest news.

5. Sheila e-mailed her mother _____ say she bought a new computer.

H CHALLENGE. WHAT ABOUT YOU? Complete the sentences, using your <u>own</u> words. Use an infinitive of purpose or <u>for</u>.

1. I log on to the Internet _____.

2. I'd buy a new printer _____.

3. I'd get a digital camera _____.

JUST FOR FUN

1 WORD FIND. Find the words listed below. The words are across (→), down (↓), diagonal (↘), and sometimes backwards (←). Circle the words. Then find the hidden message. (Hint: Read the letters <u>not</u> circled in the first four lines.)

click on	N W O D L L U P S E T R C U O
crashed	C L I C K O N U E S B L R N E
cursor	S C R O L L S H L U O R A E O
cut	T A P R O B L E E O M O S M O
file	O M I J D C P P C M R S H C D
icon	Y G T X Q L Q E T I Z R E U K
menu	R Y F E U F G R F D Z U D T A
mouse	V A O C X C T M O A J C A C D
paste	Z O B Q H J N F I L E D E J M
print	I A V L T R I S E E T S A P M
pull down	K C B W O L R P O L W C B J D
scroll	G Q O K V O P C V E W G V Z D
select	P J W N H Y T J B O X F J H F
toolbar	F C G A A F M T S O I Z Y K Q
	R C J J P G N H Z V P Z R W O

Hidden message: _____

2 POPULAR SAYINGS. Here are the beginnings and endings of some traditional expressions using <u>as</u> . . . <u>as</u>. See how many you can put together correctly. After you finish, check your answers.

as	black cold flat good old pretty quiet white	as	gold a mouse the hills ice night a pancake a picture a sheet

as old as the hills

_____

_____

_____

_____

_____

_____

Which of these sayings are similar to ones you know in your native language?

_____

_____

_____

_____

Which are different?

_____

_____

_____

_____

Ethics and Values

TOPIC PREVIEW

1 ▶ Read the letters to the advice columnist. What advice do you think the columnist may give? Check the box.

➡ Amanda's Advice ⬚ ⬚ ✕

◀ Back ➡ Forward 🔄 Reload ✕ Stop 🏠 Home 🔍 Search

Do you have any ethical questions? Write to Amanda.

① Dear Amanda:
I reserved a compact rental car, but when I went to pick it up, they gave me a luxury car for the same price. Should I tell them that they made a mistake?
Paul

Click Here for Amanda's Advice

② Dear Amanda:
My favorite shampoo had the wrong price on it. It was half the usual price, so I bought ten bottles. Do you think that's OK?
Helena

Click Here for Amanda's Advice

③ Dear Amanda:
I rented five DVDs this morning at my local video store. The clerk only charged me the rental fee for three. I didn't say anything. Should I tell the clerk when I return the DVDs?
Samantha

Click Here for Amanda's Advice

④ Dear Amanda:
Yesterday I saw someone get on my hotel's free airport shuttle bus. I know she wasn't staying at the hotel. Should I complain to the hotel manager?
George

Click Here for Amanda's Advice

---

1. ☐ Paul should tell the rental company they made a mistake and offer to pay for the luxury car.

   ☐ Paul should stop worrying and enjoy his luxury car.

2. ☐ Helena should feel great about saving money.

   ☐ Helena should go back and tell the store manager the price was wrong and pay the correct price.

3. ☐ Samantha should tell the clerk that she wasn't charged for 2 DVDs.

   ☐ Samantha should just relax and enjoy the DVDs without telling the clerk.

4. ☐ George should tell the hotel manager about the person using the shuttle bus.

   ☐ George should mind his own business and not complain about someone else.

2 ▶ WHAT ABOUT YOU? **Have you ever had a similar experience to any of these situations? Write a paragraph about what you did.**

Look at the pictures showing what some teenagers want to do. Do you think each person needs to ask for permission or not?

☐ needs permission
☐ doesn't need permission
☐ it depends (explain) _____
_____

☐ needs permission
☐ doesn't need permission
☐ it depends (explain) _____
_____

☐ needs permission
☐ doesn't need permission
☐ it depends (explain) _____
_____

☐ needs permission
☐ doesn't need permission
☐ it depends (explain) _____
_____

☐ needs permission
☐ doesn't need permission
☐ it depends (explain) _____
_____

LESSON 1

4 **Circle the correct words to complete the conversations.**

1. **A:** Where should we watch the game after work?

   B: Let's go to your house. (Your / Yours) TV is much bigger than (my / mine).

2. **A:** Is this (our / ours) room?

   B: No, we have a suite, and this is a single, so this is definitely not (our / ours).

3. **A:** Is this car key (your / yours)?

   B: No, it's not (my / mine). I don't even have a car!

4. **A:** Whose books are these? (Him / His) or (her / hers)?

   B: I don't know. Ask them if they're (their / theirs).

5. **A:** Who has traveled more? Your parents or (mine / my)?

   B: (Your / Yours) parents, I think. (My / Mine) parents don't travel much at all.

5 Change each sentence into a sentence using a possessive pronoun.

1. The shaving cream is George's. _The shaving cream is his_____.

2. The hair spray is Judy's. _____.

3. The toothbrushes are Amy and Mark's. _____.

4. The razors are George's. _____.

5. The shampoo is everyone's. _____.

6 Look at the pictures and complete the conversations with possessive adjectives or possessive pronouns.

1. **A:** Excuse me. I think you forgot something.

   B: I did?

   A: Isn't that cell phone _____?

   B: No, it isn't. It must be _____.

2. **A:** Is this _____?

   B: No, it's not _____.

   It's _____ tip.

3. **A:** Is that book _____?

   B: No, it's _____ book.

4. **A:** Are these earrings _____?

   B: No, they're not _____.

   They're _____.

LESSON 2

7 Read the conversations. Summarize the advice with present factual conditional sentences.

1. **A:** I don't have antivirus software.
   B: You shouldn't surf the Internet.

   If you don't have antivirus software, you shouldn't surf the Internet .

2. **A:** I want to e-mail some photos to my friends.
   B: You have to scan them first.

   _____ .

3. **A:** I want to make friends on the Internet.
   B: You can join a chat room.

   _____ .

4. **A:** My computer crashes all the time.
   B: You'd better find out what's wrong.

   _____ .

8 CHALLENGE. Match the two parts of each conditional sentence. Write the letter on the line.

1. If you speak Spanish, you ____.
2. If you spoke Spanish, you ____.
3. Your hair will look great if you ____.
4. If you took a taxi, you ____.
5. You'll get sunburned if you ____.

  a. don't use sunscreen
  b. could work in South America
  c. use this shampoo every day
  d. can travel all over Central America
  e. would get to work faster

9 Rewrite the factual conditional sentences in the unreal conditional. Use the true statements in parentheses to help you.

1. If we go to Russia, I'll learn Russian. (We're not going to Russia.)

   If we went to Russia, I would learn Russian .

2. If she has time, she'll read more. (She doesn't have time.)

   _____ .

3. If I need to lose weight, I'll avoid fatty foods. (I don't need to lose weight.)

   _____ .

10 Look at the pictures. Use the words and phrases in the box to complete the conversations.

too much change   undercharged   didn't charge

1. **A:** Look at this bill.
   B: What's wrong with it?
   A: They _____ us. Look.
   They _____ us for the drinks or for the desserts.
   B: I guess we'd better tell them.

1 Hamburger 3.⁵⁰
1 Cheese
sandwich 3.⁰⁰
2 Green
salad 4.⁰⁰
10.⁵⁰

W88 UNIT 10

2. A: What's wrong?

   B: I think the clerk gave me _____.
   I should have only two euros back in change, but
   she gave me twelve!

   A: I'll try to get her attention . . . Excuse me?

LESSON 3

 **Read about these people's personal values. How would you describe
each person? Write the name on the line.**

James

I love tattoos. But they
should be for men only.
Women should always have
clear, beautiful skin. And they
should just stay at home and
look after the children.

Dina

I'm not comfortable wearing
clothes that show too much
of my body.

Tessa

I think it's fine for young men
and women to get their
bodies pierced if they want to.
But if you're over forty, you
really shouldn't. It just looks
silly!

Hazel

People used to dress
formally when they went to
the opera. Now some
people wear jeans to the
opera. It's just not
appropriate!

1. Who is old-fashioned? _____

2. Who is sexist? _____

3. Who thinks modesty is important? _____

4. Who has a double standard? _____

 **WHAT ABOUT YOU? Whose personal values are closest to yours? Complete the
paragraph. Explain your opinions and give examples.**

> My personal values are closest to _____'s values.

LESSON 4

 13 Read the home page of the Internet Lost-and-Found. Then choose the best answers to the questions below. Circle the letter.

➡ Internet Lost-and-Found   ⬓◻✕

Welcome to the Internet Lost-and-Found.

The Internet Lost-and-Found

REPORT   RETURN   REWARD

If you've lost something, here's where you'll find it!

It's simple to use our website.
If you've lost something, enter your lost item into our database. Click here.
If you've found something, enter the found item into our database. Click here.

Search our easy-to-use database.

Search hotel lost-and-founds. Enter the city code here.

Search airport lost-and-founds. Enter the airport code here.

Search bus and subway lost-and-founds. Enter the city code here.

Internet Lost-and-Found Statistics Worldwide

Lost Items: 48,806
Found Items: 19,819

Lost-and-Found Story of the Week

We were on vacation when my daughter lost her gold ring. She looked everywhere but could not find it. She was very sad about it. Then she went to lostandfound.com and entered it into the database. One day later, someone called. A hotel guest found it in the hotel fitness center. My daughter was so excited. If we had waited one more day, we would have gone back home and never seen the ring again. We never met the hotel guest who returned the ring. But we want to say thank you so much!

The Jones Family

---

1. What did the Jones family lose?

   a. their daughter   b. their daughter's ring   c. their vacation

2. Where were they when they lost it?

   a. on vacation   b. at work   c. in the car

3. Where did someone find it?

   a. at the airport   b. in the bathroom   c. in the fitness center

4. If you lose something at an airport and want to find it on the Internet Lost-and-Found, what should you do?

   a. enter the city code   b. enter the airport code   c. enter the airport name

14 WHAT ABOUT YOU? What would you do if you found a gold ring in a hotel fitness center?

GRAMMAR
BOOSTER

A **CHALLENGE. Read the statements and then complete the factual conditional sentences.**

1. I usually go jogging every day, unless it rains.

   If it doesn't rain, _I go jogging_ .

2. I like driving short distances, but for longer distances, I always fly.

   _____ if I have to travel longer distances.

3. I never drink coffee after dinner. I can't fall asleep at night when I do.

   _____, I can't fall asleep at night.

4. It rarely snows here. The schools close whenever more than a centimeter falls.

   _____ if it snows more than a centimeter.

5. I never watch horror movies before bed. I just can't get to sleep!

   _____, I can't get to sleep.

B **Rewrite the factual conditional sentences in Exercise A, reversing the clauses and using commas where necessary.**

1. _I go jogging if it doesn't rain_ .

2. _____ .

3. _____ .

4. _____ .

5. _____ .

C **Choose the correct form to complete each present or future factual conditional sentence.**

1. If they _____ the musical, they _____ it again tomorrow.
      like / will like   see / will see

2. If Fernando _____ comedies, he _____ a lot.
         watched / watches   laughed / laughs

3. If you _____ some ice cream, I _____ you eat it.
        buy / will buy   help / will help

4. If I _____ fall asleep, I usually _____ a lot of work done
      won't / don't   get / got

   in the evening.

5. _____ to England if your boss _____ you there next month?
   Will you travel / Do you travel   needs / will need

6. Always _____ your seat belt if you _____ to be safe.
           wear / wore   want / will want

7. I _____ a tattoo if my parents _____ me not to.
    didn't got / won't get   tell / told

8. If I _____ my mother for permission, she _____ no.
      ask / will ask   say / will say

9. If I _____ far, I always _____.
     travel / will travel   fly / flew

D Use the moral dilemmas to ask and answer questions, using the unreal conditional.

1. **Moral dilemma:** You found someone's credit card in a restaurant.

   Q: _What would you do if_ _____ ?

   A: _If I_ _____ .

2. **Moral dilemma:** The drugstore didn't charge you for some items.

   Q: _____ ?

   A: _____ .

JUST FOR
FUN

1 Complete the sentences. Then put the numbered letters in order. You will write an English proverb.

1. Those shoes are my shoes. Those shoes are __ __ __ __ .
   ⎯⎯1⎯2⎯⎯

2. When there are different rules for different people, it is a

   __ __ __ __ __ __   __ __ __ __ __ __ __ __ .
   ⎯⎯⎯3⎯⎯⎯   ⎯⎯⎯4⎯⎯⎯⎯⎯⎯

3. Lipstick, eye shadow, and mascara are all __ __ __ __ __ __ .
   ⎯⎯⎯⎯⎯5⎯⎯⎯6⎯

4. Another way to say "you're welcome" is " __ __   __ __ __ __ __ __ __ __ __ ."
   ⎯⎯7⎯⎯   ⎯⎯⎯8⎯⎯⎯⎯⎯9⎯⎯⎯

5. Another way to say "absolutely" is " __ __   __ __ __ __ __ __ __ ."
   ⎯10⎯⎯   ⎯11⎯⎯⎯⎯⎯⎯

6. When someone has ideas from the past, we say he or she is

   __ __ __ - __ __ __ __ __ __ __ __ .
   ⎯⎯⎯⎯⎯12⎯⎯⎯⎯⎯⎯⎯

   Proverb: " __ ."
   ⎯12⎯10⎯2⎯5⎯9⎯4⎯7⎯⎯1⎯9⎯⎯4⎯12⎯5⎯⎯3⎯5⎯9⎯4⎯⎯6⎯10⎯8⎯1⎯11⎯7⎯

2 Think of five different ways to reply to "Thank you." Write them on the lines below.

1. __ Y __ L __ (○) __ __ __ E
2. __ __ N' __ __ __ N (○) __ __ __   I (○)
3. N __ (○) A __ __ L __
4. __ O __ R (○) __ __ E __
5. __ (○) __ ' __ E __ __ L __ O __ __

Now unscramble the circled letters above to make a word.

This is something teenagers should get permission for. __ __ __ __ __ __